Praise for Genie Zeiger's *Atta Girl!*

Genie Zeiger's lovely memoir of her childhood brings us back to a vantage point we all once shared but perhaps have lost, to a time when the world was still new and full of wonder, and where we were seduced by our own need and freedom to question.

—Aryeh Stollman, author, *The Illuminated Soul*

If you were a Jewish girl in the fifties, if your mother ever said, "Go do something constructive!," if you loved your library and wondered about God, you will adore this book. And if you were none of the above, but want to laugh right out loud while reclaiming a big dollop of your innocence, *Atta Girl!* will take you there. Genie Zeiger is Anne Frank at a safer, simpler, sweeter time.

—Nancy Slonim Aronie, Author, *Writing From the Heart*

What is life anyway? Everybody wants to know. In this fine book, Genie Zeiger reveals her secret desperation to understand everything and everyone, including God. Like all 12 or 13 year olds, she fears nobody will tell her all that she needs to know. So she calls in Mr. Imagination and pretends her mother, father, and rabbi have agreed to sit and answer any question. Take a delightful, funny trip with Genie who grew up to become a published American poet, with answers for almost everything.

—Barbara Beasley Murphy, author, *Miguel Lost & Found in the Palace*

Atta Girl!

A Memoir

By Genie Zeiger

Sherman Asher Publishing / Santa Fe

In memory of my parents, Ruth and Carl Zeiger, and in honor of my children,
Mara Silver and Josh Silver

Library of Congress Control Number: 2005925474
ISBN: 1-890932-27-2

Sherman Asher Publishing
P.O. Box 31725
Santa Fe, NM 87594-1725
www.shermanasher.com

Edited by Nancy Zimmerman
Design by Jim Mafchir

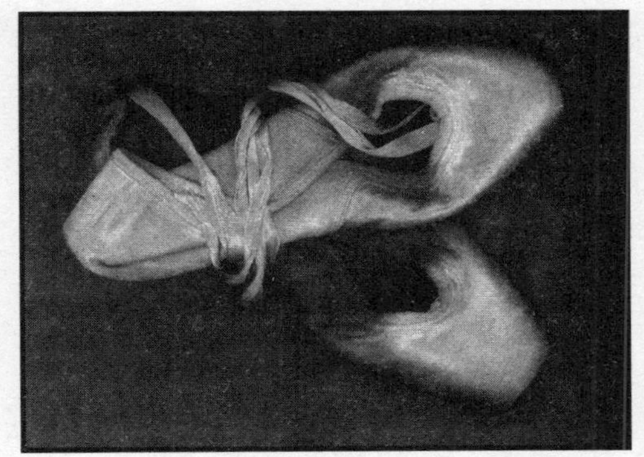

1

I don't understand what God is, I don't understand what life is. What kind of a life is this for a kid? I am so full of questions, I'm going to burst. What can I do with them, where will they go? That's what I'm thinking today as I sit in our little, little living room. My mother is making supper, as usual. The parakeet is swinging on his perch, as usual. My father is at work, as usual, and my sister, Susie, I don't know what she's doing, and I don't care so long as she isn't bothering me. I'm bored, as usual, and I begin wondering if God made the world because He was bored too. I have so many thoughts, and no one to tell them to; I have so many problems, and no one to discuss them with. Somehow I know no one around here really wants to know what I'm thinking. I guess that's just the way life is here, in Queens, New York.

"No man is an island," I read in a poem, but I feel like an island, and I'm not a man either, I'm an eleven-year-old girl. "Each girl is an island," I write in the back of my school notebook. I don't understand why it is that whenever you have one kind of a person or another to represent everyone, it's always the boy. Then, as usual, I give up thinking, and pick up one of the books I've gotten from the Steinway

Public Library, *Green Mansions*. I get into my favorite reading spot on my bed with my back to the wall, stick my fist in my cheek, lean over my book, and jump in. Suddenly I'm in a very lush forest. I hear monkeys screech, leaves rattle, snakes hiss, and I'm not me anymore, I'm Rima, the forest girl, half naked, half normal, and the star of the book. I'm also the hunter who loves her and is running around trying to find her. I am everyone and everything, like maybe God is, but He hides like Rima. I mean where do you see Him? And what do you call Him? In Judaism, the rabbi says, you are not even allowed to say His name, it's not possible, so you call Him lots of things, none of which is really his name. This makes communication difficult. Now the Christians think that God is Jesus Christ, but the Jews don't. It's kind of strange because Jesus was Jewish, and a carpenter, like my grandfather on my father's side who died from TB when my dad was three years old, which is sad.

Anyway, the great thing about reading, unlike thinking, is you can escape. Today I decide that I will write stories and help other people get a break from their boring, frustrating lives. Of course, I love libraries, and in fact, I think that our library is even better than the Astoria movie theatre, which is pretty great. We walk to the movies on Saturday afternoons, our money rattling in our pockets. There is a strict matron there who never tells you her name; I think that helps her be mean because without a name you can't really know her, or make fun of her in any personal way. Anyway, this matron is the movie boss and she gets you and your friends to sit down by waving her flashlight towards the seats *she* decides you will sit in. If you're late and the lights are out, her flashlight is fun to watch, but it's kind of silly when she uses it with all the house lights on. Maybe she's pretending to be the Statue of Liberty and the flashlight is her portable torch.

I always bring a book to the movies. My mother thinks this is ridiculous.

"What do you need a book at the movies for?" she always asks me as I'm leaving the house.

"Because...." I let out a big sigh. "You know," I say.

The reason is that if I'm early for the movie, I can ignore my friends and read my book for a few minutes until the lights go out.

°°°

The library, which is near the little orthodox synagogue I am forced to go to, is even farther away from our house than the movies, and I have to take the Q19A bus to get there. I get out at the last stop and cross Steinway Street to the Steinway Library, which is new and big. I always have seven books to return, and I always take out seven new books to read—you never know, you might not like one or two of the books you take, so it's a good idea to have a selection. I have a notebook with a long list of books I've read including authors, titles, and number of pages in it. I also add the date on which I finish the book. The list now covers two and a half three-hole composition papers.

The librarian, Miss Rose, knows me and always smiles. What she doesn't know is that I'm ruining my eyes (that's what my mother says) and making dinner late because of all the reading I do, because I always yell, "Just a minute, I have to finish this chapter," when my mother calls me to the table to eat. What she also doesn't know is that I'm ruining my teeth too. I can't help it, it's how I like to read—cross-legged, the book in my lap, my fist pushing my teeth in on the right side.

I hand my books to Miss Rose, who always asks, "And how are you today?" I smile and say, "Fine." Then she always asks, "Did you like your books this week?" And I say yes even if I didn't like some of them. I don't want her to feel bad, the books are kind of like her children.

The books I don't like are usually the boy kind of books where ships collide or spaceships burn up or an airplane crashes. Always terrible, loud things happen in them. Like in the Bible with the Canaanites killing the Methodists, or whoever. Now, action and adventure is okay, but the problem is that you don't get to know the characters, and that's what I like, characters. Maybe it's because so many people in my neighborhood are boring. If I get a good character to read about, it's much more exciting than explosions and accidents because I can go into their minds, and their minds become very real, even though I can't draw a picture of a mind the way George Insana, who's in my class, can draw a car on fire.

In the library, I head for the fiction section, which is all nice and tidy with authors' last names from A to Z. I walk up and down the aisles looking for good titles. This can be tricky because you have to tilt your head all the way to one side to read them and your neck starts killing you. But it's worth it. Sometimes I look for the classics. They all have the same kind of important-looking covers—Charles Dickens, Nathaniel Hawthorne, Louisa May Alcott, Emily Bronte, etc. The ladies usually write about characters more, and so I mostly choose them, although I did think *The Scarlet Pimpernel* and *The Hunchback of Notre Dame* were great, and those are more in the boy category.

I get so excited when I'm in the library that sooner or later I always have to go to the bathroom, which is embarrassing. Sometimes I have to race there, but first I have to ask Miss Rose for the key. At that point, I'm usually ready to mess my pants, and so I ask her really fast, like I'm crazy, but it's just my nerves from the excitement of all the books.

The Jews are said to be "people of the book;" we even kiss prayer books after they accidentally fall down. I don't mean we get on our knees to kiss them, we pick them up first and then kiss them, like we do after we touch the Torah with them. Maybe loving books and being Jewish are related.

If I become a poet, I will write poems to books because I love them much more than boys, so far. I love their smell—papery and gluey. Even the old ones, the ones no one has taken out for years, (you can tell by the dates stamped in the back), I like their old smell, like Grandpa's study, or the books in the synagogue, which are really old because God Himself, in all His glory, wrote them. I love the sound of the crack of the binding when I open a brand-new book. I love being the first to take it out. I even like the shiny plastic Miss Rose, Mrs. Dinnerstein, or Mr. Morris put on over the new covers in order to protect them. They're a lot nicer than the grocery bags my mom makes me cut up to use to cover my schoolbooks.

A library is a quiet place, a secret place. You can hide between the stacks and no one knows. You can get lost inside a story—fly to China, be poor and dream of rice; you can be a forest girl, or French, or a guy with a long sword. You can steer a ship or plant a tree in Brooklyn or watch your true love die or save a person's life.

My mother says I inherited my literary interests from my grandfather, who never wrote a real book, but writes poems and made an invention, which is, I think, similar to writing a book. His invention is this: You put a sprayer into the lid of your garbage can so that every time you throw something out and close the can, the lid shpritzes off a nice smell so your garbage isn't stinky and you don't mind taking it out. I think that if my grandfather keeps using his imagination, he can make a whole book of his ideas and it would be in the card catalogue, maybe under "Inventions," but of course, with his name, "Greenberg" in the author section. I know a lot about the Dewey Decimal system.

P.S. 2 Gene Zeiger
5-1 Oct 7, 1953
My Ambition
When I am older
I would like to be
a poet because I am
pretty good at poetry.
I will go to college
Her are some of the
poems I made up.
1. Come Dear Child
Come Dear Child come
and see what your
father has for ye
beautiful doll
beautiful hair just
for a child so cute
and fair. For you
are full of so much
charm that to you
will come no harm

When I get older, I want to write a book for kids, and then maybe some bored girl like me will take it out of the library and get so excited that she, too, will have to go to the bathroom. Then she'll take it home and sit on her bed cross-legged, ruining her eyes and teeth, but she'll love it, the book I mean. And when she's done (in one day of course), she'll put it on her book list, with my name in the author column. And Miss Rose, very old and gray by then, will take the book from the girl's hand when she returns it, and she'll ask this girl, "Did you like the book?" And the girl will say, "Oh, yes, this one's great," and she'll hold up my book. And her smile will be so big that Miss Rose will look at the name of the book, *The Secret of a Girl's First Heart,* and the author's name, Genie Zeiger, and she'll say. "I knew her...my, my." And the girl will drop her mouth open really wide and say, "You did? You knew Genie Zeiger?" And Miss Rose will sigh, a faraway look will come into her eyes, and she will tell the girl about me and how when I was a girl, just like her, I came to this very library. And the girl will say, "Wow!" and "Gee!" and look at the cover of *The Secret of a Girl's First Heart* like she's looking at her first real boyfriend.

2

Books are made of stories and everyone loves a good story, so here's one that's true. When I was five, I was taking a bath with my little sister and she made a doody, and there it was, number two, floating between us, closer to me than to her. "NO FAIR!" I screamed to my mother.

"Of course, it's not fair," she said. She had just run into the bathroom as fast as she could after she heard me yelling. She got me my Jack and Jill towel, wrapped it tight around me, and sat me on top of the toilet seat, closed of course.

"Yucky," I said, "Very yucky."

Susie's doody was still floating in the tub and she was just sitting there staring at it, what an idiot.

"I think you better get her out," I yelled. I was still pretty upset.

"Relax," my mother said, "just relax."

"I can't, it's too yucky. I want a shower."

"You can shower after Susie's out."

Mom got Susie out, then scooped the number two out of the tub with some tissues, washed us both in the shower, and then scrubbed the tub. She never once said "Ugh," she just acted like a janitor.

"Susie's little," she said to me later in the kitchen, "she

didn't mean it."

"I'm never, never going into the tub with her again."

"Okay," Mom said, "you don't have to." She was washing lettuce and making salad. We are always eating salad. I was sitting on the wooden dining-room floor under the birdcage. I was hoping that our parakeet, Rin Tin Tin, wouldn't do a number two on my head and wondering why God, who is supposed to be "all knowing," lets bad things happen. Maybe He just can't keep up with everything—I mean there are millions of people in the world running around doing things…billions, and so lots of awful, strange things happen. I remember once, when we were walking down 79th street, an airplane flew so low I had to hide on the sidewalk under my sister's stroller so it wouldn't hit me. Then I thought about how, when I was four, I threw up on the backseat of Uncle Manny's brand new Oldsmobile. I thought of our neighbor Janet's polio, and of Mr. Clifford, who lost his legs in the Korean war. I thought about all these things until I couldn't think anymore. I wish God would explain things to me. I keep talking to Him and all I get is silence, airplane noise, or my sister pestering me.

"I'm going out to play," I told my mother.

"Okay," she said, "but come back soon please." A circle of carrot she had just cut rolled off the counter onto the floor. I picked it up.

"Let me rinse that for you," she said, "there might be germs."

I handed it to her and she ran it under the faucet, then gave it back to me. I popped it into my mouth and headed out.

It was getting cold, and it was cloudy, not a very nice day. I didn't see any of the kids on my block, not one. I walked toward the corner. Where was everybody? A plane flew overhead and I watched its silvery body lower itself toward La Guardia airport. I wondered if I would ever, ever get to go somewhere besides here.

Then Linda Solomon walked out of her building with her little pink Spaulding rubber ball. I wondered what kind of mood she was in. It could be bad.

"Hi," I called in a cheery voice as she headed down the three steps to the sidewalk. She didn't answer, just bounced her ball in front of her. What a rat.

"What's the matter with you?"

She ignored me.

"Baby, baby, stick your head in gravy," I said and ran towards my house.

I turned around to see what effect it had, but she didn't even look up from her ball. What a double rat.

"Back already?" Mom asked.

Sometimes she asks pretty stupid questions. *No, it isn't me, it's my identical twin. No, I got hit by a car and it's my ghost. No, it's President Eisenhower.*

I decided to ignore her, the way Linda ignored me, and went to my room, which felt as empty as the streets.

3

Because we live right near an airport, airplanes are a big deal in my life, but so far I've never flown in one. When I was in the third grade, Miss Hinchey took our class to La Guardia and a man in a navy blue suit and a blue cap with wings pinned on it led us up a ramp to look inside a DC 7. It was okay—fancy and shiny—but I was surprised at how little the windows were; what's the point of flying in the sky if you can hardly see anything from up there? Although it was interesting, it was not great because the plane just sat there. Kind of like my life. Kind of like my parakeet's life. What is life anyway? The rabbi is supposed to know, but when he says important things, he says them in Hebrew, and I only know a few Hebrew words: *Adoshem* is God, and *Yerushalayim* is Jerusalem and *Melech*, I think, is holy or king, I'm not sure. And even though I don't know what I'm saying in Hebrew, the grown-ups make me say those words anyway. It's so strange—that's why sometimes I wonder what is life and why did God make it this way?

Of course, I don't wonder out loud. What for? My mother would say, "Do something constructive, make Jell-O." My father would say, "What?" then he'd fold his newspaper the fancy long way we learned with *The New York*

Times in school. My sister knows absolutely nothing. Who can you talk to about important things? I tried testing God again yesterday because I was bored, but He didn't answer. I stood in my boring room staring out my boring window looking out at the boring street and I said, "God, if you exist, make a miracle." I didn't say it loud, but softly because the "Holiest of Holies," that's what we call him, is supposed to hear everything, even your thoughts, so why waste your energy?

What I did next was I took a deep breath, held it, and counted to eighteen, *Chai*, a holy number for good luck. I stared out the window and do you know what? Nothing happened except Mrs. Bell, our downstairs neighbor, walked out to her white Ford, took out the key from her black handbag, opened the car door, sat down inside, and shut it. I thought, this is not a miracle, but then I decided to think more about it. I sat down on my bed, crossed my legs and thought and thought—certainly this did not compare with the burning bush in the Bible, or with a bit of oil burning for eight days for Chanukah. Then I wondered: do miracles have to include burning? Once I burned my finger, but no one thought it was a big deal, even though I did because it hurt so much. If Mrs. Bell's hair caught on fire while she was walking, now that would be a miracle.

What are miracles anyway, and why are they so important? Maybe they only happened a long time ago when God was younger and had more energy to make them happen. My mother says being born is a miracle—but if being born means you're alive, and this is life, the "b" word, "boring," then I need to think this over some more.

4

One way to avoid boring is: Bam! Crash! Bam! Although breaking things is definitely embarrassing, I keep doing it. Moses did it, he broke the tablets with the ten commandments when he got mad at the Jews who were doing some dance around a golden calf. I don't know what got into them long ago, and I don't really know what gets into me, but it's something and my mother's getting fed up. She's saying I have "ulterior motives." I tell her I don't have ulterior motives, but the truth is I don't know what an ulterior motive is. If I asked her, she'd say, "Look it up in the dictionary," and she'd say this in a very snooty and superior manner, like she does whenever I ask her what a word means. It's as if she's too important to take her precious time to explain "elaborate" or "diffident" or "caustic," which are some of my vocabulary words this week. You'd think the dictionary was the Bible; it even has a real leather brown cover, and pages as skinny as my sister, which my father once told me are called "onionskin." My parents keep the dictionary in their bedroom on a shelf so high I have to get on tippy toes to reach it.

After I think about it, I decide that my ulterior motive with breaking things dates back to sucking my thumb. This is why: I really liked to suck my thumb until I was ten, which is pretty old, but who cares? It didn't hurt anyone, only my teeth, which got stuck out and so I had to suffer and get braces. But that was after I had to suffer a long time with something else called Thumbs Out! which is brown and tastes like sour poison; it's worse than Passover horseradish in the bitter department. I wonder who took his precious time to invent such a thing? The point is that I think I began breaking things because I was really mad at my mom because she painted that stuff all over my yummy innocent thumb over and over, ruining it with her ideas. Maybe that's why I knocked over the stand with the lamp on top, two ashtrays, and a donkey with a plant on its back. The donkey broke its neck and the dirt went flying all over the fancy, flowery living room rug.

"I didn't mean it, not at all," I told Mom as I picked up the donkey's head with the little straw hat, "I'm sorry, I really am." She picked up the lamp stand, glared at me, and said nothing, which is worse than something because with something at least you know what it is. I decided to stay down there on the rug on my knees and pretended to be busy cleaning, but really I was poking little bits of dirt between the long pink wool threads so she wouldn't see what a big mess I made. She hates dirt, and that's a problem because she sees it where no one else does. She is the president of The Society for People Who Hate Dirt. She even thinks that water is dirty because she wipes up little drops of water inside the sink with a yellow sponge.

"Water's clean," I mention, watching her.

She doesn't answer, she just keeps sponging and squeezing.

"The blinds are clean," I say when she asks me to dust them again.

"Oh no they're not," she says, then marches to the

window, takes her finger and runs it over one of the metal slats the way I would with chocolate icing inside a bowl, if she ever baked desserts like some of my friends' mothers do. Her priorities are strange. And I'm not so dumb that I have to look up "priorities" in her precious dictionary.

The next breaking incident was really bad because it was on a major scale and it wasn't in our house, but in our neighbor's, Selma Solomon's. Selma is my mother's friend. She is tall, blonde, and very pretty. If she were president, it would be for The Society for People Who Love to be Pretty and who, instead of cleaning, like my mom, try to make themselves beautiful all the time. One night I went to sleep with my hair in rollers and this really hurts because of the weight of your brain and head which press the metal wires into your scalp when you lie down for sleep and a good dream. That night Selma came in to say "sweet dreams" to my sister and me because our parents were out at meetings. I said to her, "I hate rollers, God do they hurt."

Selma straightened her back and looked at me very seriously and said, "Suffer for beauty." Her voice had a little lilt to it, but she meant it, I could tell by her eyes. Then she breezed out the door and left me to my headache and intended beauty.

So our family was at Selma and David's for dinner, with their daughters of course, Bonnie the slow one and Linda the rat, and my job was to dry the dishes with Linda. I remember they were white with pink roses. I remember because that night I managed to knock over not one dish, or even two, but an entire dish drainer full of dishes. I think I did it with my elbow or something, but I'm not sure. Selma didn't get mad at all because I was really upset and began to cry. My mother rushed into the kitchen, but she didn't say anything to me. I started to try to pick up the pieces as fast as I could so I wouldn't have to see my shame, but the mothers both said, "Be careful, you'll cut yourself," and shooed me out of there. Then they began to discuss what happened, and I heard them.

"She's always knocking things over." That's my mom. "I'll reimburse you for all of this, I'm sorry, this is terrible."

"Don't worry, Ruthie," Selma said, "it's nothing." The two of them bent down, swept and gathered the pieces as if they were in some famous field, like Moab's in the Bible. But it was only Jackson Heights, only a tiny apartment, only my life's mess they were sweeping up—pick, pick, pick. I didn't care that much, but I did. They were really pretty dishes with all those little pink flowers.

ooo

Losing things is also something I do well. Maybe that's a Jewish thing too—I mean the Jews wandered around in the desert for about forty years; maybe they lost their way. As for me, I lose objects. First my pocketbook at the Lincoln Memorial, then a whole pile of books, some from the library. I left those on the bus. Hats and gloves are really easy.

"It's a wonder you don't lose your nose," my mother jokes.

"Ha, ha." I say. What I think is that my nose is too big to lose, just like hers and Dad's.

"Mom, I'll try not to lose or break things anymore, I really will," I said to her one day. She was sitting in the living room sort of crying. She's never sick and she never cries, but there she was on the couch, wet-eyed, with a tissue in one hand. On her lap, in a little nest of other tissues, was our parakeet, Rin Tin Tin, with his green feathers, dead. Mom felt worse than I did, but I felt bad, and bad for her because she was crying. That's why I told her again that I'd try not to lose or break things anymore. She smiled and motioned me to sit next to her, which I did. She smelled good. She put her arm around me, and her arm is a little fat even though the rest of her isn't and it felt good when she held me, like it would with Aunt Jemima. We both sat and looked down at Rin Tin Tin. It was pretty sad, I mean he just lay there dead, his little black eyes open. No more flying, no more pecking at seed, doing number two, or stepping onto my finger. No more anything. I sighed. Mom sighed.

"I love you," Mom said, stroking the bird's wing.

"I know," I answered, because even though she was looking at our bird, I knew she meant me.

That night Susie, my dad, and I buried Rin Tin Tin. First I wrapped him in more Kleenex. I made a design of it—blue, pink, and white tissues in layers. Then I flattened some of them all around the inside of a gray and green Stride-Rite shoe box and used only blue tissues to make a blanket since he was a boy. He looked cute and comfy with only his little head and beak showing. I let Susie lay him down in the box, then we both closed the lid and Dad dug a hole near the playground with a shovel he borrowed from Mr. Berman, the superintendent. We threw the dirt back into the hole in handfuls, then Dad shoveled the rest on top and patted it down with the bottom of the shovel.

"Ashes to ashes, dust to dust," I said, like I heard in the movies. I didn't know what Jewish people said at funerals because kids aren't allowed to go to them.

"What?" my sister asked.

"Ashes to ashes, dust to dust," I snapped.

"That's dumb."

"No, it isn't!"

"Yes it is." She looked at my dad for confirmation, but he was jiggling the shovel, trying to get all the dirt off it so it would be nice and clean for Mr. Berman. He's also a member of the Clean Society, but my mom says he's really more neat than clean.

"Why is it dumb, smarty-pants?" I asked her looking down at her dumb, dirty blond hair.

"Because it's feathers, not ashes, feathers!" Then she stuck out her skinny arms like wings and pretended to fly away.

"It's poetry, stupid," I called out as she ran towards the apartment behind our dad, "poetry!"

Dad said, "Come along," but I stood there alone for a little while and recited, "If I should die before I wake, I pray the Lord my soul to take." Then I sang "Oh beautiful for spacious skies," because I like how the "amber waves of grain" part sounds, although I can't really picture it. I walked back to our house and went in. My sister was begging my mother for a dog again, working up to a big scene, and so I went to my room, shut the door, and tried to think about what life was since I'd just seen something dead. It was all pretty confusing. The clean part and the beauty part, the dead part and the part that always wants something new, like a dog. That part, the wanting, I decided, was really the life part. "Dead" meant you couldn't want anymore, and so I made a list of things I wanted:

1. Toe shoes
2. Grimm's fairy tales, my own copy
3. A new shirt like Jane Farrell's, with puppy faces on it
4. Never to die
5. To stop losing things
6. Peace in the world
7. My father to talk to me
8. A red bedspread (I hate the brown one)
9. A different sister
10. A break from dusting

5

Having a sick sister is not a good thing, especially if you have to live in the same apartment as her, in the same room in that apartment and so you can't get away from her, except when you go to school. Then there's how she looks—skinny with a chest that sticks out like a chicken's after Dad carves off the white meat. It might be nicer to say her chest looks like a tent, but the chicken metaphor is more accurate. If she's your sister and you look normal, you feel proud in comparison, but also guilty, and your mother makes you feel that way too because any complaint you have, like a stomachache, or a worry that your nose is too big, or that death scares you is nothing like bad asthma. What I mean is you just know you can't say these things to your mother because your sister needs the attention, not you. A big nose is just a deal on your face, and a stomachache goes away, maybe you just ate the wrong thing, like moldy milk. And the idea of death, well, I can imagine Mom saying, "That's so silly, you're a healthy young girl." What I don't hear her say aloud, but do hear inside me is, "We don't ever talk about big important things, philosophical things, we just talk about homework and clear the table and please dust the venetian blinds, how was school and have you finished your homework?"

Having a sick sister is like having a sick dog who sleeps in your room right near your head and wakes you up wheezing and gasping, then sits there like a pick-up stick on her bed until she finally gets Mom into the room with something on a tray. Our mother looks like a ghost in her white nightgown and her hand, which is in a white cotton glove, because she has Lazar's paste, whatever that is, on for her eczema, whatever that is. I have to lie there awake watching this night after night, like a bad television show. Sometimes I even wish I had asthma, which is stupid I know, because asthma can kill you, but at least I'd get some attention, and instead of turning my foam-rubber pillow over and over for some coolness, I could say, "Mom..." real slow and whiny, and she'd sit next to me and say, "What's the matter, honey?" and I'd say, "I'm scared," and she'd rub my back gently, not hard or bone crack-y like the chiropractor, and ask, "What are you scared about?" And I'd tell her how scared I am of death because Susie's trouble breathing makes me feel as if death is in the house, like a neighbor, Selma, or Muriel, I mean a real live person, and that it will take me away, not Susie, and there will be nothing and nothing is scarier than anything.

And then she'd say, "It must be hard to sleep in this room hearing your sister," and instead of going back to her bed with Dad, she'd lie down with me, her arm around me, and I'd listen to her nice, even, peaceful breath and breathe with her and fall asleep calm and unafraid. But that never ever happens. I don't say any of that; she doesn't do any of that. Instead, she gives Susie some medicine, which makes her awful noises a bit less awful, and I lie there scared and shut up with all these ideas running inside my head like crazy bugs.

Having a sick sister might be easier if there were another healthy sister or brother in the area, but Mom once said she decided not to have any more kids because Susie came out so sick. That was the one and only time she ever mentioned it—sick. An icky word, an icky sister. Not her fault, I think. Yes, I think, all her fault.

The problem with feeling plain shut up is that the things that need to get out, your own feelings and your own thoughts, just stay in there, like a bone in your throat, and you can't chew it up like my Aunt Toby can. What I mean is she doesn't exactly swallow bones, but she bites into them, chicken bones I mean, and then she sucks out the marrow, which is the brown and red inside. This is almost as disgusting as eating the *pipik*, the belly button of a chicken, or a tongue, which, I recently realized, really is a tongue from a cow's mouth.

Sometimes you can call something by its name and have no idea what it really is. For years, tongue had nothing to do with a real tongue. My dad would, at Mom's request, which sounds like a command, get the slicer, like in a deli, put this pink blob on it, start cranking a knob and slice it up. I'd watch and never, ever realized, despite the yucky bumps on the end of it, in spite of the shape, how it tapers like the small version in my own mouth—forget it, it's too terrible. Maybe more terrible than death, which is what I started out thinking about.

So I sit up in bed sometimes and listen to my sister try to breathe and get scared to death, which is a pretty accurate saying. Not like, "See you next year!" which I say a lot, but then, one New Year's Eve, I said it to my parents who were all dressed up and ready to go out, Mom in her Persian lamb coat and Dad in a navy suit. Suddenly, "See you next year!" was a true saying, and I was stunned, like the truth hit me on the head.

Maybe I wouldn't be so scared of dying if I was Christian and I thought I'd go right to heaven. But I'm Jewish and the rabbi doesn't ever talk about where you go after you die, drop dead, or "pass away," which is the polite way of saying it. I wish I could ask him, but I'm just a kid, and he's too busy.

So the sad part—and I do feel sad about it even though I'm always supposed to feel happy because I have food, clothing, parents, a place to live, blah, blah, blah—is that I sometimes sit on my bed so scared that there aren't words for it. Death feels like nothing. And I don't know how to make death into something okay. It's terrible trying to make something out of the idea of nothing. And so I sit there on my bed and I don't cry, I just turn myself into something hard, like Lot's wife. I think of how awful and miserable it is to imagine I don't exist at all. It's not the death thing, I mean I've seen flowers and parakeets die and it seems kind of peaceful. It's the nothing part that gets to me—not to be me, or anything. It's so alone that there aren't even words to get close to it. It's all air, emptiness, nothing to touch. And so I hold my blanket—I'm too old for a doll and God forbid I should put my thumb in my mouth—and all this falling darkness is there, and this empty feeling that makes me wonder if God exists at all. Because if God made the world and me, how in the world could I possibly feel so much nothing? How can the psalm I read once in synagogue say the world is "without end" when everything dies?

Well, what happens is that I get to the point where I can't stand thinking about this anymore, and go back to the list of things I want, which is taped to my desk. I go to number one, toe shoes, and decide to really pray for them, although I'm not sure about praying. The rabbi says it's how you talk to God, and so, of course, you do that in synagogue. Most of the time you tell Him how great He is, then you apologize for all the bad things you've done, and beg for good things to happen. When I tried praying at home (not out loud, of course, but in bed at night when I think God must be resting too and might hear me better), it didn't work. Maybe God is like my father, too tired to be interested in me. Anyway, I really, really wanted toe shoes, pink, satiny ones. I begged my mother, but she said, "Ask your dad." Then I begged my father and he said, "Ask your mother." Then I begged my mother again, and she spoke to Fara Lynn, the dance teacher, who said I wasn't ready, so I tried praying to God again and realized that praying feels the same as begging, and what's more, nothing happened. No wonder. For one thing, God is a man, like my father, who always says, "Ask you mother." If God were a woman, maybe I'd have a better chance.

ooo

Here's where Miss Marsh, our sixth-grade teacher, comes in. First let me tell you that she hides a bottle of whiskey in her desk, second drawer left. She is shorter than most of us, and usually wears the same light blue dress with a white shiny belt tight around her tiny waist. One day, in her same old outfit, she gave us a talk about bootstraps. It was a cloudy winter afternoon, almost three o'clock, and we were all ready to dive into the coat closet to grab our jackets, hats, scarves, mittens, and boots. There were a few minutes left before the bell rang and Miss Marsh stood up on a chair and said, "Children, I have one more thing to add." That was strange because we'd been reading aloud and had finally finished our book about a kid named Tom Sawyer, so I had no idea what she'd be adding to. Maybe it was just one of those things grown-ups say to sound important. A kid would never say, "I have one more thing to add," she'd just say it. I was curious though because Miss Marsh's tone became very serious, like she was selling Colgate toothpaste, or announcing a war.

"If you want things to happen in your life, don't expect someone else to do them for you. Lift yourselves up by your own bootstraps, rely on yourselves, your own natural resources, to get ahead." I thought natural resources were things like oil or diamonds in Peru, I never thought of them as fuel or jewels inside my own body. Then she told us, for the hundredth time, about how she grew up in a poor family without a father, and how her mother had to hem skirts until two in the morning. I hate when she tells us this story because I feel so bad for her mother…her fingers must have killed her. Fortunately, the dismissal bell rang before Miss Marsh got to the worst part about her older brother, Frankie, who got run over by a trolley when he was twelve.

I decided to let the other kids grab, tease, and torture each other in the clothes closet. When only the slowest kid, Diane Di Mitzio, was left tying her pink scarf around her neck, I put my coat on, stepped into my brown galoshes, and walked out of school. My friends had left without me, and I was glad because I had thinking to do about toe shoes and how to get them. I decided Miss Marsh's advice was good, and that maybe God made her give this advice today as a sign. I decided that if I saved up all my allowance, birthday and babysitting money and maybe sold a few things, like pencils, I could get seven dollars, what toe shoes cost at Macy's. I only had eighty cents so it was going to be an ordeal. Then I remembered what Gail Benson, my sort-of friend, said, "God helps those who help themselves." Now,

I don't like that sentence, it sounds too certain, but you never know until you try.

Maybe I was being vain, about the toe shoes, I mean. Only Elise Lapinksi and Diane Shecter, the very best dancers at Fara Lynn, had them. Then I decided that I didn't care why I wanted them, I only wanted them. "Why?" can be a dumb question sometimes. Like with my three-year-old cousin, Robert. You say, "I'm going to the bathroom." He says, "Why?" You say, "Hi, Robert." he says, "Why?" You say, "Do you want me to read the Jack and the Beanstalk book to you?" and he says, "Why?" and hands it to you.

°°°

It took me a whole year to save up for toe shoes, and even though I only got to $5.65, my father said he admired my perseverance. "Atta girl! Here's two bucks," he said, and I had $7.65. My mother took me to Macy's, a store so big it's really like a city, with blocks of cosmetics, sweaters, hats, you name it. The shoe department is so big it carries every kind of ballet shoe. My mother and I waited until a tall lady dressed in a pale blue suit with a wart on her nose came up to us. She didn't look at all like a dancer, which was disappointing.

"May I help you?" she asks, dipping her head down so that I could see how her wart was not a regular circle, more like an oval. Of course, she talked to my mother, not me. I'm just a kid. She had no idea that I was the one who slaved and didn't buy malted milk shakes so I could be standing in front of her seeing up close how ugly her wart really is. My mother tells her that her daughter Genie wants toe shoes.

"Pink ones," I add.

"Please follow me," she says, turning to a line of pale blue leather chairs with fancy wooden legs. My mom and I sit down.

"I will measure your foot first," Miss Wart reports, then gets the big metal measurer. I stand up like I do for Mr. Mitchell in our neighborhood Stride-Rite shoe store. Miss Wart squats, resting on one knee, then squishes my big toe down. She puts on her glasses, which had been hanging on a silver chain around her neck, and reads the size. She doesn't say the size, she just says, "Hmmm," which makes me nervous. Then she gets up and disappears behind a curtain that says "CAPEZIO" in bright pink letters.

My mom fiddles with her purse. I can tell she thinks Miss Wart is a big shot, but I think she puts on airs. I can tell because a big shot would not be bending down like a slave on her knees in front of a young girl in Macy's. She comes back with three boxes.

The toe shoes are really beautiful, as beautiful as I imagined. Perfectly pink and shiny. The long ribbons are sleek and match just fine. This is my idea of beauty with a capital B. Better than mountains or trees.

We decide the size 5 fits, and I pull them on to check once more and get my heel tucked in the back. Then comes the best part: Miss Wart wraps the ribbons around my ankle and up my leg. I feel like a real princess, but I can't get the full effect yet because she won't let me take off my brown socks because of germs. I can only imagine how great it will look when I get home and put them on with my pale pink tights.

Thank God my mother doesn't tell Miss Wart about my perseverance, economy, etc., about how it took me a whole year to save up the $5.65 and how I stuffed all my money into a little manila envelope, the kind we put milk money into at school. Mom pays, and Miss Wart puts the green box in a nice Macy's bag. She even smiles a little when she hands it to me. Maybe she's not such a bad lady after all.

I hold my package carefully on the subway ride home. I think of all the fairy tales where someone gets what they searched and searched for, like a magic apple or a bag of gold, and then someone or something takes it away. There's a bad-looking man across from us on the train: he's fat and he's wearing a red, greasy cap with the word "YANK" on it in black letters. His nose is running and he is not wiping. His belly sticks out from under his jacket. He could be a robber, so I hold my toe shoes close to my chest and nestle a bit behind my mother's brown fake fur coat. I close my eyes between stations so I don't have to see him; I notice my mom does the same.

We're finally home and I can unwrap my toe shoes and put them on. I can really get up onto my toes. My arches curve beautifully and my feet are really ballerina feet now. I can't wait until ballet class on Thursday. But when Thursday comes, no one says much or seems excited, maybe because they are jealous, or maybe because I'm not one of the best dancers. A few of the okay dancers say, "Boy, are you lucky!" and Fara Lynn lets me be in the first line during one of the "across the floors."

ooo

Unfortunately, this story, such a happy, pink and satiny one, has a bad ending. "God," my mother says, "works in strange ways." This is what happened. It wasn't the dirty man on the subway, it wasn't fairy-tale magic, it was that two weeks after I got the toe shoes, my feet grew a whole size. I wished I was a Chinese girl with bandages on her feet so it could have been prevented. I tried and tried to force my feet back into the shoes, but they just wouldn't go. I prodded and poked day after day. I cried. My mother tried to stretch the slippers, she took them to Mr. Messina, the shoemaker, and he tried. I even let my sister pull on them, but they were just too small. Then I hung them on the wall above my bed so that I could see them and in my dreams, maybe, I could still be a ballerina. Everyone was nice to me, even my dad. But nothing could be done. No Prince Charming, no fairy godmother, nothing. How could my feet do this to me? Sometimes awful things happen, and what can you do? Nothing. "Maybe you just weren't cut out to be a ballerina," Dad says, patting my head. Maybe he's right, but I'd never say so.

God obviously does let bad things happen, but I confess that toe shoes not fitting is nothing compared to the Holocaust. I'm ashamed to even put them in the same sentence, which I just did. Like everything else really important in this world, no one ever talks about the Holocaust, but I have a nose for it, I found out. First I found this book in the library about a girl named Anne Frank who was Jewish, like me, and lived in Europe and had to hide because these bad Germans called Nazis wanted to kill her. Why? Because she was Jewish. It's crazy to think that people with blond hair mostly want to kill girls (and boys and grown-ups) because they have brown hair mostly and are Jewish. Anne Frank looks so much like me (I saw her picture on the front of her book) that I couldn't believe it. I stared and stared and got a creepy feeling in my chest, like she was me and I was her, which is crazy, but that's how it felt. Maybe also because, like her, I want to be an author. My best friend is Italian and she's blonde, but I don't feel like we're the same even though we talk about our secrets sometimes. I can't figure it out, this thing with Anne Frank, but I stared at her picture so long we became friends, which is another big mystery that no one can explain and so why even bother trying? Another big thing my parents don't know about me.

This is what I'd like to say to my mother: "Why don't you tell me all about the Holocaust, which was happening when I was growing inside you and you were smiling and happily listening to Frank Sinatra, or the show *Oklahoma!* We don't live in Oklahoma, we live in Queens. I know that a tree grows in Brooklyn, where we used to live, before we moved here, but what about the Holocaust that is in my chest along with Anne Frank's face?

I bet my mother says nothing because she doesn't want to upset me. But you know what? I think she really doesn't want to upset herself because if I'm upset, she is. I feel this, like it's the truth, the way I feel Anne Frank inside me. These things make no sense, but they do. It's like poetry, which I love. In poems, things are not logical, like Walt Whitman saying, "I am the grass, I am the woman doing laundry, I am the Negro in the furnace room," etc. So with poetry, I could say, "I am Anne Frank." And this is true, even if I couldn't explain it in an essay for school, or to anyone.

So what do I do? The usual. I read books. I read Anne Frank's diary and feel like I am hiding in an attic, even though it was too sad to really imagine, and then I think of people being put in gas chambers after their jewelry and other stuff is taken away and put into big piles. Can you believe such things? I can't stand even killing ants—it's cruel to squish the life out of them, like Joey Fioretti does for fun. People. People killed. And sadly, that train of thought leads right back to God. If God made us, and loves us, how in the world could He let something like that happen to us? How can God: 1. Create people who could even think about killing other people? 2. Let them do it?

I did read another book called *Twenty and Ten*, which made me feel a little better. It's a picture book about twenty Christian kids and a nun, Sister Gabrielle, who, like all nuns, looks like a penguin. They are French and help ten Jewish kids, who the Nazis are looking for, by hiding them in a cave. They share their food with them even though they don't have much. Eventually, they fool the soldiers and save the lives of the Jewish kids. I didn't know the French did things like that—I thought they drank a lot of wine, ate long bread, and spoke a beautiful language.

I know that history is full of horrible stuff because of boring social studies classes where you have to memorize dates of wars—1776, 1814, 1914. But all of that seems long ago and far away and does not, so far as I know, involve a girl who looks like me, a girl who is sensitive and smart and wants to be a writer. So here I go again with questions and no one to ask them to.

There is one special man who seems like a good God to me, and his name is Mr. Danziger. Mr. Danziger takes care of the synagogue and is there a lot of the time. He has numbers in blue-green on his arm, near his wrist, and he is, I know from my reading, a Holocaust survivor. I would like to go up to him and touch his numbers and tell him how sorry I am, and that I know something about what he went through because of reading. Then he could tell me what happened to him, and I would listen. I know he lost his wife and his son because Arnie Rosenberg told me this after he heard his mother talking on the phone one day. He whispered it as we were running up the stairs to Hebrew School and Mr. Danziger was, as usual, smiling at us with eyes that looked like houses full of love, saying, welcome *kindeleh*, as we walked in the door and he patted our backs. I thought, I wish God were like Mr. Danziger. Then I thought, maybe He is, the way I'm like Anne Frank. Then I got a feeling that was like drowning, so I threw the idea away, like a wrapper to a piece of Double Bubble gum.

My dad is the silent type, not lovey-dovey, and sometimes that's really nice, like now while my mother keeps "oohing" and "aahing." Just because we're seeing mountains and trees doesn't mean it's heaven. Jews don't talk about heaven like a place to go if you're good, but Mom keeps at it, as if it were heaven on earth, telling me to look at this—Wow! Look at that!

Big deal, a tree. Big deal, a mountain. Her voice gets phony, which I hate, although it's true: The trees are nice, really big and wild compared with the scrawny ones that dot our block at home, and yeah, a mountain is really greater than an apartment building. Moses went to the top of a mountain, Mount Sinai, and saw God, I remember this, but the more my mom exclaims, the more I can't help mumbling, "What's so great about that?"

"What did you say?" Mom asks, turning around and looking at me over the back of the front seat.

"Nothing."

I pretend to be looking out the window, but I'm closing my eyes and in my mind I'm still saying, "What's so great about that? What's so great about that?"

Dad just drives along with his left arm out the window, the yellow hairs on it blowing in the passing wind. With his right hand he clicks his ring with the black stone on the steering wheel in time to *Singing in the Rain*, which he is humming. Maybe he's happy not to be at work. So, to make a long story short, he's humming, and I'm "What's so great-ing" so I will still feel like me, and not the Little Miss Nature Girl my mother wants me to be. She doesn't trust me to appreciate beauty on my own, and so she goes ahead and ruins it. If she keeps this up, I'll live in the city for the whole rest of my life, which is very long, and I'll never see a really big tree or mountain again. And if she likes trees and mountains so much, what's she doing living on 79th street between the Grand Central Parkway and Ditmars Boulevard?

My sister is playing with her patent leather pocketbook in her skinny little lap. At least *she's* quiet.

Then we drive past trees that are really green and gigantic in one long row. Maybe Johnny Appleseed planted them.

"Just look at those evergreens!" Mom says, turning her head in my direction. "Aren't they beautiful?" My dad is now humming *Over There, Over There*. Susie looks up from her pocketbook for a second, then fiddles with its fake gold clasp. My mother is waiting for someone to agree with her. I can't stand it another second.

"What's so great about that?" I yell, "What's so great about that?"

My mother turns to me and looks me straight in the eye. "What?" she asks.

I repeat, "What's so great about that?"

Dad stops humming and clicking. Susie stops fiddling with her clasp. All I hear is the wind the car is slicing and the hiss of tires. It's like the silence in school when Miss Shannon, the principal, suddenly walks into the classroom, a quiet filled with important things people would like to say but don't. My mom turns back and stares out the windshield. The beautiful trees and mountains are still there on both sides of the road, quiet and large. I keep saying "What's so great about that?" to myself inside my head, Any minute my mother is going to start up again in that awful tone of voice. Dad begins humming and clicking his ring to *Oklahoma*, which is tricky because it's a complicated song, and my sister is inching her stupid pocketbook closer and closer to my side of the backseat. Soon there's going to be a big fight in this little car.

7

Another place we often drove to when I was younger, and not old enough to go to camp like I do now, was Rockaway Beach .

"Lucky us," my mother always said at the door of our tiny bungalow, which was in a row with a lot of other little bungalows. They looked like the small green houses in Monopoly, but they were gray. Every day we packed up stuff to take to the beach, and everyday my Grandmother said we schlep too much: three folding chairs, a yellow and white umbrella for the sun, a basket with cream-cheese and jelly sandwiches on rye bread, lots of fruit, and a mayonnaise jar full of orange juice. My mother always put a piece of waxed paper between the jar and the lid so the juice wouldn't leak out. We also brought towels and a soft pink and white faded flannel blanket, which used to be on my bed. I didn't like seeing that blanket there on the sand with shoes on each of its corners to keep the wind from blowing it away.

I also didn't like the crowds of people there, like Macy's but without the shopping. There were naked legs and arms and chests and backs all over the place. There were shovels and pails, and towels and chairs. It made me wonder what the Jews took with them out of Egypt when they crossed the Red Sea. I mean we're not rich or anything, but look at all we take for one day, and those Jews were going away forever.

One day my sister and Milton Ezrati left our blanket, and with all the legs and body parts all around us, plus all we schlepped, you can understand why no one noticed they were gone. Then Edith, Milton's mother, said to my mother, "Have you seen Susie and Milton?" My mother, who was lying down for a change, sat up fast. My first thought was "WOW! Something is happening!" But quickly I got a little butterfly in my stomach—the beach was really, really crowded.

I wonder how Susie and Milton even found room to escape between our blanket and the blue one that belonged to another family only two inches away. That family didn't care about Susie and Milton, they were busy arguing about wet bathing suits. "You'll catch cold," the mother said to the daughter, even though it was at least 100 degrees. The mother had a dry bathing suit on because does she go in the water? No. Does she have fun? No, parents don't believe in fun. So the mother wanted her little girl to take off her wet suit right then and there, and this was a huge problem because of embarrassment. I know a lot about that because my parents have a home movie of me taking a bath, which they show to company. This mother said to the girl, "Off," and the girl said "No," and began hitting the sand with her fists, which could have been dangerous if she had a cut and the sand got in it and caused an infection. Anyway, the mother won because that's what parents do, and she held a towel around the waist and legs of her daughter who stared off into outer space with a very bad expression. I knew she was thinking that everyone was watching her, so I turned away when the hard part came, which is trying to pull a dry bathing suit up a wettish body under a towel that's not big enough and you think everyone is going to see your tush or your vagina.

My mother was still looking for Susie and Milton. Susie could be identified by her chest which, as I said, sticks out funny, like a chicken's, because of her asthma. Milton just looked like a normal four-year-old-boy, but his mother Edith is not normal because instead of bending down on her knees to wipe the kitchen floor, she throws a rag down and smushes it with her foot, which I think is very original. Edith went to look for the kids in one direction and my mother went in the other.

I'm embarrassed to admit this, but I didn't really care if they found those two or not. Actually, I thought it would be a miracle if they did find them because of all the towels and people and blankets, which looked pretty much the same—same worried mothers in dry bathing suits, same fathers reading newspapers or sleeping, all the brothers and sisters running around kicking sand into everyone's sandwiches and eyes or sitting and digging.

The ocean is really big. When I stared at what seemed to be the end of it, where the sky and water met, I imagined a gigantic waterfall there, the water cascading down to somewhere as far away as Japan. But did anyone ask me about Japan? Does anyone wonder about interesting things like imagination? No, it's just eat this, wear this, do that. Fathers get tired working in an office all day, and mothers get tired at home dusting, cooking, shopping, getting their hair done, ironing, and telling you to go to sleep. My mother always says, "You have to go to sleep at eight o'clock, or you'll get sick." But I don't get sick, even if I go to bed at nine. After I thought all of this through, my sister was still lost in the middle of a million blankets and two million people on one long piece of sand. Just when I thought it was all over and I was an only child, there they were—my mom with Susie on one side and Milton on the other. The kids were smiling, my mother was not. The excitement was over and now I had to wait for something new to happen.

Sometimes I think the sky is falling, and that is an event. It isn't true, of course, but I think so anyway. I'm not Henny-Penny, but we live right next to the airport, and having huge metal things take off and land down your block can be pretty scary, and annoying. When the television is on, you have to watch people talk because you can't hear a word they say, and when you're on the telephone you have to tell your friend, "Just a minute please," hold the phone to your ear, stare at the wall, and wait for the racket to end. Sometimes the whole apartment shakes.

Some afternoons I walk to the overpass above the Grand Central Parkway near the runway. That's when my heart really falls into my stomach, or even further down to where you don't say. I stare down at the cars zipping under me and wait for planes to zip over me. When planes go over your head and cars go under your legs at the same time, it feels really strange, like the whole world is having a contest to get somewhere fast.

If it's a sunny day, airplanes make you squint because metal reflects light. Sometimes I shut my eyes completely to protect them and wait for all the racket to stop. Then, when I open, it's like coming out of the movies in the afternoon—what a surprise: the whole world is lit up, same as it always was. I have also noticed that there is a special second when, if you open your eyes just a little bit, then shut them quick, it's quite thrilling, I don't know why. And I don't really like using the word "thrilling" because my mother uses it in a phony tone of voice about things we see, nature mostly, when we go on a trip, or driving to Aunt Gertie's, but I can't really think of a better word for that moment when a plane is flying toward you, passes over your head, and you look up at its shiny belly, then turn around fast to watch it put out little metal things that slow it down. Then it lands. The 707s can land on short runways and that's why they're so special: this is what my friend Diane's father, Mr. Benson says, and he should know because he's a pilot.

9

My parents have lots of friends who are not pilots but who dress up and get together. My mother even has a mink stole for these occasions. It is brown and, of course, furry. I don't like the word "stole," it sounds criminal, and "mink stole" is a strange combination of words.

Where do they go, Mom in her stole, Dad in his suit? They say they are "going out." They say my sister and I are old enough to be alone, that there are neighbors in the building. Susie and I stand in the living room and watch them leave in the dark outside our window, Mom waving as Dad dives down the stairs. Then we watch television, play Monopoly, Clue, or read. We have milk and whole-wheat cookies (my mom thinks they're healthier than real ones) while they're out with the crowd: Julia and Rollie, Arlene and Jessie, Ellie and Phil, Sylvia and Ray, all their old friends.

ooo

One night the crowd comes to our house. I'm already in my pajamas when they arrive. I look in the living room and they are laughing, eating, and drinking liquor, Scotch or rye. The women have very red lips, and say, "Come here and say hello." They smile, pat and kiss me because I am Ruth and Carl's. The men are kind, with soft bellies and nice smells. Then they talk, talk, talk to each other and I go to bed and listen in the dark to the click of the ladies' mah-jongg, and the slip, slap of the men's pinochle. I smell cigars and perfume as I fall asleep.

I know they're going to eat the pineapple triangles off the fancy colored toothpicks, which leave blue or pink stains in the holes after my mother stabs them. I know they will munch the raisins and walnuts which I helped Mom put in fancy little cut-glass dishes. Later I know she will take out the good white china with the gold trim and serve coffee and cake because she told me they always have coffee and cake at eleven o'clock. The morning after they visit, Sunday, the house feels different, like friendly ghosts are in it even though the crowd is gone.

On Sundays, my cousin Ira and I play a dress-up game, Bungida-Bongida, at Grandma and Grandpa's. Grandma has a big box in her bedroom, which she keeps under her bed with its bumpy white bedspread that leaves marks the shape of strawberries on your legs if you sit on it too long. The box has great stuff in it: Grandpa's tall black hat that he wore to his wedding to Grandma, his old glasses, Grandma's shoes, lots of scarves, and some dresses my mother says are "out of style." She always wrinkles up her nose when she says this, like "out of style" smells bad.

Except for the food at my grandparents' house, it's boring, and so Bungida-Bongida is very important, so much so that I start thinking about it when I go to bed on Saturday night.

At our house, every day is pretty much the same—I wear the same sorts of things, eat the same kind of red Jell-O, string beans, meatloaf, etc. But, thank God, Bungida-Bongida is never the same. Even though my cousin Ira is a boy, when we dress up you can't even tell who's the boy and who's the girl. We put on a *lot* of stuff, sometimes two hats—a black one with a veil, and a red one, like a box, on top of the black one. Sometimes there are three scarves around our necks, and two around our waists; sometimes a shirt becomes a pair of pants that are hard to walk in.

Getting dressed up is a kind of magic, a glamour. You look in the mirror and have no idea who is looking back at you—it could be an angel, or one of the Everly Brothers. You could even stare at yourself and say, "Who's that?" but that would be carrying things a bit too far. You know it's you, of course, but the exciting part is that it's also not you. You never look *that* crazy! But because now you really do look crazy, you can't say the normal things grown-ups like you to say such as, "Hello, how are you?" and so you scream, "Bungida-Bongida!" standing in one place, like you would if you were saying the pledge of allegiance, or telling your mother that her friend Selma called and she should call her back.

After we are all dolled up, Ira and I run into the living room where the parents and grandparents are talking. The men talk to the men, and the women to the women. Why? I don't know. It seems that a lady and a man talk to each other only if they're married, but my parents hardly talk when I'm around and sometimes I wonder why they got married at all. I mean they do dance together to Sinatra after dinner sometimes, but mostly they don't seem to be good friends. Maybe it's because Dad is so tired from working all the time. Maybe it's normal for married people with kids just to do what they're supposed to do, and that's it. For Mom: cook, clean, go to meetings, shop, tell us what to do. For Dad: work, read the newspaper, carve up chickens, turkeys or tongues, do chin-ups on a bar screwed between two sides of a doorway, and sleep.

Another thing that keeps them apart, I think, is that my Mom is religious and Dad is an agnostic. Mom loves going to synagogue and Dad hates it, I can tell by the way his face gets screwy on holiday mornings when we are getting ready to leave for Beth Jacob. To him, Jewish holidays are like Mother's Day or Father's Day, "commercial." Commercial is bad; this has something to do with capitalism.

I think my dad loves me, but I'm not sure because he doesn't talk to me. Then I think that maybe he *does* love me because he always says, "Atta girl!" which to me equals saying, "You can do it," which equals, "I believe in you." My father is like a can of peaches, sweet but hard to get open. How do you know if someone loves you anyway? By their eyes? By what they do? What they say? I think it's mysterious and nothing you can prove as fact. My heart feels that he loves me, and, as I said, I know he's always tired from working six days a week so maybe he just doesn't have the energy to show it.

But getting back to playing, to Bungida-Bongida—when Ira and I run into the living room, sometimes tripping because of falling scarves or shoes that are too big, or shoelaces untied, all of the grown-ups stop talking, which is a miracle because grown-ups always talk. They stop like in freeze tag and stare. It's a great moment, just a quick itty-bitty second when we can be anything to them—Martians, or strange animals never seen before on earth. It's a great moment, like when you're in the candy store or at school and you hear someone say, "Hi Genie," and you don't know who it is, so there's still a surprise in the air. But then it's only Gail Benson, or someone else who is boring. After the Bungida-Bongida moment, the world gets busy again, the grown-ups go back to their normal talking all at the same time, and Ira and I run away, throw the clothes off, and start over. The best part is that it's exciting again, like another chance to ride the merry-go-round free after you've reached out and grabbed the gold ring—you, you got it!

10

One spring, we drive down to Washington in our new two-tone Chevy, turquoise and white. As usual, my dad has his elbow out the window and tap, tap, taps on the steering wheel with his gold and black ring.

My father loves to scare me when he's driving. How? Easy—he takes both hands off the steering wheel. "Dad, stop it!" I scream. I'm in the backseat next to my sister, of course. I can see his face in the little mirror and he is smiling. Why he thinks this is funny, I don't know. "DADDY!" Finally he puts his hand back on the wheel, clicks his ring a few more times and stops smiling. "Thanks a lot," I say like I mean it, but I don't. Why should I thank a grown man, who is my own father, for driving with his hands on the steering wheel?

My mother has a different problem. Hers is with her arms, the upper part. She drapes the left one across the top of the front seat between her and my father and all this stuff hangs down. It's really the only place she has fat, as far as I can see, and it jiggles when we hit a bump, it jiggles when I flip it around with my thumb and pointer finger slowly, the way you'd try to get a dead goldfish out of the fishbowl. It is strange that an arm, especially your mother's, can be controlled this way—I can make it roll like a wave at the beach, or I can make it fall like a fat pancake. At first my mother ignores me, maybe because she feels sorry for me since she knows I hate my father's steering-wheel routine. My mother is very fair and respectful. She also believes she is the master of right and wrong, like Grandpa, her father, who reads the Bible so much. Anyway, she lets me jiggle her arm. Maybe she thinks it's sort of funny too. My sister does. She tries the arm routine after me, but then Mom gives us the evil eye. "Enough!" she says, laughing, then adds, "You'll probably have fat on your arms too one day—genes."

°°°

I can see why Washington, D.C. is such a big deal. Everything is white and stony and clean: the Washington Monument, the Supreme Court, the Lincoln Memorial. I always liked President Lincoln, even before I saw his beautiful statue, because he freed the slaves, and I don't believe anyone should be a slave to anyone or anything else, the way the Jews were slaves unto Pharaoh, or I am sometimes a slave to my father's driving with no hands on the wheel. I mean what can I do if he's in charge? It helps me understand why the slaves in the south wanted to go north to somewhere safe. That's why they sang *Swing Low, Sweet Chariot*.

It turns out that the bad thing about Washington is the Washington Monument because I leave my pocketbook there, in the bathroom. It is a huge one in the basement with tall green walls and big toilets with cracked black seats, the kind that have two arms which don't reach all the way around to meet each other. There's a long chain you tug on to flush. I have to put my pocketbook on the floor so I can pull the chain, but then I leave it there with two dollars, a hankie, and a white comb inside it. My parents take me back the next day to try to find it, but no cigar. I wonder who took it? Who is so poor that they need my pocketbook?

My mother says, "You're always losing things." It's true, and I don't know why, it's a mystery, like God or a mirror is a mystery. Maybe some girl I never saw took it and maybe she's spending my money right now.

11

Grown-ups think saying hello and good-bye is a very big deal. "Kiss Grandma good-bye," or, "Say good-bye to Mr. Mitchell." Mr. Mitchell is the Stride-Rite shoe man and I know the top of his head better than I know his face because he bends over when he measures my feet. I stand up correctly with my heel pressed back against the end of his measurer, and he squishes my toes down in front with his fat hand to check my size, both the long way and across, just like Miss Wart did. All I see is the top of his head, and he has three freckles there, which make me think of dark stars because they are in the middle of his bald spot which is like a little sky. After she pays for the shoes, my mother holds them in one hand, her navy blue purse in the other, and says, "Say good-bye to Mr. Mitchell." I say, "Good-bye Mr. Mitchell," which makes me feel like a parrot.

I don't like hellos that much either, but they're better than good-byes. In school, they taught us how to greet people politely with introductions: "Gail, this is Eddie; Eddie this is Gail." All that stuff. With hellos there's something new that could be great, like opening up a new book that you can't stop reading. I hate saying good-bye to really good books; I hate getting to the last page and having to close them. It's like stopping eating something very delicious, or not finding your favorite sweater at the playground after you've gone back to look for it because your mother says, "Sweaters don't grow on trees, go back and find it." But it's

Books Read Since July, 1957

1-	Imperial Woman	346	Buck
2-	So Big	360	Ferber
3-	The Patriot	372	Buck
4-	Grapes of Wrath	619	Steinbeck
5-	Rebecca	457	Du Maurier
6-	Auntie Mame	254	Dennis
7-	Showboat	398	Ferber
8-	Come My Beloved	311	Buck
9-	Pavillion of Women	316	Buck
~~10~~	~~The Citadel~~	~~401~~	Cronin
11-	Figure in the Dusk	211	Creasy
12-	Scapegoat	348	Du Maurier
13-	Helen Keller	166	Brooks
14	Burning Bright	159	Steinbeck
15.	Green Pastures	173	Connelly
16	Cyrano De Bergerac	256	Rostand
17	Tea and Sympathy	182	Anderson
18-	Carousel	168	Hammerstein
19.	Gone With the Wind	1067	Mitchell
20-	Bonjour Tristeisse	127	Sagan
21-	Native Son	359	Wright
22-	My Fair Lady	186	Lerner
23-	East Wind: West Wind	169	Buck

gone. And it's not good to lose money either, because then you have to babysit a long time to get it back and babysitting can sometimes be the "b" word, "boring."

Did you ever notice how when you have to leave your friend's house because it's suppertime and you're in the middle of a great game of Monopoly how there's this tiny second when you stand up getting ready to leave and your heart falls a little bit inside your chest? Maybe a quarter of an inch, maybe an eighth, just a teeny bit, but you feel it. Same with finishing a Hershey's or listening to the ending of a song that's number one on the hit parade, the kind of song that gives you goose bumps and makes you want to jump up and go wild. When it's over, your heart sinks a bit.

This makes it really hard to imagine dying. I mean you suddenly have this gigantic good-bye to say to everything. There must be a little second, like after my father swats a fly with his newspaper on the screen and it jiggles on the windowsill, a tiny moment after its little leg, the one that was moving last, stops—that second. I hope God is the one you see after that happens, when your heart drops probably at least a foot, or maybe six feet because that's how deep they dig in the ground to bury you.

My mother says God is our Father and it must be true because why else would there be all these churches and synagogues and temples not only in Queens, but all over the world, in India, China, Canada, etc? I mean there couldn't be all those fancy expensive buildings for nothing. So when you die, I like to think God is the one to open you back up like the book you've written by living it, the book you've become when you're old. That He opens it up, I mean opens *you* up again and is happy to see you, like your parents are, most of the time. In our synagogue, if you drop a book by mistake, you have to pick it up and kiss it—it's that terrific and important. And what I think is that a person is even more terrific and important than a book, because a person is the one who writes the book.

12

When I was younger, we'd go visit Uncle Larry and Gertie a lot. I remember thinking that just because she's my aunt doesn't mean I want to see her. But what can I do?

It's a long drive from where we live to Aunt Gertie's house, and it's on a stupid windy parkway with lots of stupid cars and lots of stupid trees. My mother begins her "Isn't it beautiful?" routine the minute we pass the sign with blue letters and two Indians that says "Westchester County."

My father stops the car in the circular driveway when we get there. "Well, let's go in," he says. This is when the real trouble begins because Aunt Gertie has a dog. Now, I think dogs are basically okay, even though I saw a bad one bite my friend Michael on his lip when we were both about three...actually, now that I think about it, I hate dogs. I hate that little black and white dog because it bit Michael on his lip. And I hate Aunt Gertie's dog because it's bigger than a dog should be; it's big as a bear and its name is Rajah, not Roger, which would be normal, but Rajah, like he's something important. Would you believe this dog is called a boxer? I do, because this dog is really like a boxer, one of those big guys who beat each other up. But this boxer doesn't have another dog to beat up or try to kill, so it tries to get me.

Will my father carry me in? No. "You're old enough to walk," he says. So I sit in the car after he, Susie, and my mom go in and Rajah has jumped and growled at them. I've seen that black stuff around his mouth that looks like liver with yucky little dots of pink on it. It looks like his heart is right next to his teeth.

After a while I get sick of sitting in the car because it either gets too hot in summer or too cold in winter, depending, but I sit there anyway until my father takes pity on me and comes out to get me. He tries to do what he thinks a good father would do: "You're a big girl," he announces. That's a really stupid thing to say. Sure, I'm bigger than I used to be, but if I'm still small enough for him to carry me into Aunt Gertie's house so Rajah won't jump all over me and give me a heart attack, why not? That dog is a lot bigger than me. Just because Aunt Gertie is his older sister doesn't mean he can't ask her to tie Rajah up. I always end up crying, which I don't like, and out of breath from running beside my dad who keeps saying, "Atta girl! C'mon, it's okay, atta girl!" as Rajah keeps jumping up at me until I make it to the door.

Aunt Gertie gives me real coffee with lots of milk in it. Like this is my reward for being jumped on. At home my father always says coffee stunts your growth. My mother watches me drink. At home she's really bossy, but here she's like a mouse. Aunt Gertie is rich and I think this is why my mother is quiet. When we visit my poor cousins in their tiny apartment that smells like garbage, my mother talks a lot.

Aunt Gertie's house is ten times bigger than our apartment and it is dark. It smells old and musty, like it gets no fresh air. I want to go out, but outside is Rajah. So I stay put. I'm like Jonah in the whale, but I'm sure it smells even worse inside a whale than it does in here.

What are we doing here anyway? Why do grown-ups do the same things over and over again, like going to work, going to sleep, cutting their toenails, brushing their teeth, and visiting relatives? Why don't people just do what they want? I can't, but my mother could. She can drive, so why isn't she driving over to see Frank Sinatra, who she loves so much? Why doesn't my dad go dance with Ray Bolger who he loves so much? Why do interesting things only happen in books or at the movies? How will I ever have an interesting life? And now how will I get back to the car without Rajah biting my feet and ruining my chances for a career in dancing?

13

"Don't be mean!" my mother says when I tell my sister she's stupid. What's so bad about being mean? God was mean sometimes, like he was to that nice man, Job. Another time was when the Jews were wandering around the desert with Moses and they got sick of eating manna, which is strange because manna is supposed to be heavenly food, but they wanted meat. Poor Moses felt so bad for them that he went to talk to God about it, and do you know what happened? God made it rain meat in the form of quail, which is like chicken. All these dead birds started falling from the sky, like a storm. There were so many that it was a problem, stepping around them and trying not to get hit on the head by one.

Rajah is mean, but he's a dog so it must be instinctive. I know meanness is the opposite of being nice, but what's so great about being nice? If I'm supposed to be nice to everyone all the time, that has to include being nice to me, which means that sometimes I have to be nasty because it feels so nice to me. Besides, I've noticed that if you act nice all the time, the meanness gets clogged up inside you, like the toilet does if it isn't flushed.

For example, take George Insana in Miss Brisbane's

French class. He's always waving his arms to make trouble, and she keeps pretending that he's not acting up. So he keeps at it, getting crazier and crazier because she's not putting her pretty hand on her pretty hip and saying, "Now, George what is it?" Before you know it, George is standing up, holding on to his desk, reaching up and waving so hard that he looks like a crazy sailboat in a crazy storm. Of course, by now the whole class is staring at him and not listening to Miss Brisbane's explanation of how to conjugate the verb *être,* "to be," and this may become a major low point in Miss Brisbane's teaching career. If she had paid attention to George sooner, she might have avoided this. With being mean it's the same. Just throw in a few "Idiots!," a few pinches, and you may prevent a bigger scene later on.

My mother once did something uncalled-for, and I know she really enjoyed it. She was mad at me for telling her to shut up, so she stuck her hand into the penny jar on top of my dresser, grabbed a big handful, and threw them at me. I couldn't believe it, but there they were, hundreds of pennies, falling all over my bed and floor. It was great! I began humming the song, *Pennies From Heaven*, which my father likes to sing. My mother froze for a second, listening to me and looking around at the mess. Then she left the room really fast with her hand over her mouth because she was laughing.

In books there are lots of evil people, and in movies there are monsters, criminals, liars, murderers, and cheats. So, really, what's so bad about a few "shut ups" or "stupids?" Sometimes I wish I had the nerve to do things more criminal than breaking and losing things. I have a friend, Gail, a girl in my building who does—she steals candy from Mr. Chessler's candy store. She has freckles and big teeth, but she's pretty in her own sort of way. What she does, in her pretty sort of way, is to stand in front of the long and wide case with the Milky Ways, Lifesavers, Chiclets, Nestles, Hershey's, etc. as if she's trying real, real hard to make up her mind which one to buy. Then she looks around like a nervous rat to see if anyone's watching, and if they're not, she jabs her hand out, grabs something and sticks it into her jacket pocket. How do I know all these details? Because once she made me do it with her.

"C'mon," she said, "it's fun."

I was scared and not convinced of the fun part. Mr. Chessler is definitely the king of his store. He wears a white apron with stains on it that make him look like a butcher. Also, my mother would kill me if she knew I stole things. One of the Ten Commandments is "Thou shalt not steal. "

"Gail, I can't," I say. We're walking to Chessler's and getting close. I see the green awning, I imagine the heavy glass door getting bigger and bigger.

"C'mon," she says.

I follow her in, I don't know why, then stand next to her in front of the candy. I watch her out of the corner of my eye, like a spy. *Whish*, she does it—M&Ms. It's so fast and easy, I can't believe it. I'm really nervous now as she keeps hissing, "Do it, do it!" Then, without even looking to see if anyone's watching, which is pretty dumb, I grab a Milky Way and try to whisk it into my pocket, like she did. Wouldn't you know it—it gets caught on my pocket half way in and half way out so I have to shove harder and harder and it makes a crinkly noise when I finally get it in. I think I'm dead. But nothing happens.

"Let's look at the comics," Gail says, all casual. My legs feel like my red wooden stilts in the closet at home, stiff and dead, but I follow and stand next to her as she casually picks up the new *Little Lulu.* That's when Mr. Chessler looks over.

"No reading comics in the store, girls," he says over the head of an old man bent over his coffee cup. Lots of old men go there and drink coffee.

Gail looks up, smiles sweetly and puts it back. "Sorry, Mr. Chessler," she says. What a snake.

We leave the store. The sun is bright and it takes a while to get used to it. again. It's April and spring is finally here. I wrote a poem about spring last year:

Spring is here, spring is here
With the sky so bright and clear.
Birds will sing in the trees,
And there will be a pleasant breeze.

"See how easy it was?" Gail says. She has her hand in her pocket, wrapped around her prize. I don't say a word. She starts talking about Tony Gilbert, this kid with red hair who she has a crush on.

I don't tell anyone about the candy, I throw it down the incinerator, which is pretty stupid when you think about all the trouble it took to get it. A few days later, Gail says, "Let's do it again!" like she's asking me to play hit the penny, like it's totally normal.

"No thanks," I say loudly and firmly so she'll get the message.

ooo

I just wasn't cut out to be a thief because I can't help feeling really bad about the candy, although I didn't even eat it. I've come to the conclusion that I'm cut out to be mean once in a while, but only in the word department, not in the stealing department. I feel bad for Mr. Chessler, who works in his store all the time and always looks tired. I think how great it is that I can decide to do this and not that, to make my own kind of life (unless my mother disagrees). I will never ever steal again. I know that being "good" gets boring, but mostly it's okay. I'm deep into these important thoughts when my sister comes into the room and asks me for a pencil. I'm being a philosopher, and she is interrupting my important chain of ideas, my questioning. If no one will answer my questions, I have to try by myself. "Will you shut up?" I yell at her. Then I hear her running to the kitchen to screaming, "Mommy, Genie was mean to me!"

14

When school is out, the summer days before I leave for camp are really dull. But sometimes you get a good one, like when the Good Humor man came twice in one day. The first time was eleven in the morning.

I run up the stairs to our apartment, "Mom! Mom!"

"What is it?' She's ironing next to the birdcage. Our new parakeet, Lassie, likes to swing and watch her iron.

"Can I have a Good Humor? Please?"

"You know you can't, you haven't even had lunch yet. Why that young man comes at this hour is beyond me," she adds, the steam from the iron hissing in her hand.

"Phooey." I'm out the door again. No one is buying ice cream. Mr. Stanley, who is too young to be a mister, keeps clanging his bell and driving his truck so slowly it could be walking. Finally he turns the corner and disappears and there's only the faraway tinkle of his bell.

Joey and Gail and Amy are out in front of Joey's building. Joey's father died last year, but he looks happy anyway. I wish I knew how his father died, but you're not allowed to ask things like that.

"Want to play skellies?" I yell from the sidewalk. "Sure!" they all yell back. It's our favorite game now, so we meet up the street between two cars that are parked far from each other, and Amy draws the outline for the game with her fat pink chalk. There's plenty of room on the street because all the fathers and their cars, except Joey Fioretti's, of course, are at work.

Skellies is fun, but you have to be really careful not to skin your knuckles. This is how it goes: You draw ten little boxes with the numbers one to ten written inside them along the sides and in the corners of a big rectangle. The object is to flick your bottle cap from one to the next, in order, until you get to ten. There are only three flicks allowed for each turn, and whoever gets to ten first wins. This time it's a really good game because Joey and I are both very close to winning. I really want to beat him, I always want to win, that's how I am. Anyway, just as I'm about to make my move from nine to ten, the big truck with the Tilt-a-Whirl on it starts coming down the street. "Hey!" Joey shouts.

The Tilt-a-Whirl is a ride, the kind you usually have to go to an amusement park to find, but the great thing is that that this one finds us. Six kids get to sit on each side, strapped in, of course, for safety's sake. The best position is at the top because when the Tilt-a-Whirl really gets tilting high, you're really up there and you feel like you might go over the top, fly off, and get killed. It's cuckoo that the things that are the most exciting and fun can almost kill you. Everyone likes the Tilt-a-Whirl better than skellies, so we all quit the game and run to our mothers for dimes. My mom will give me one, I know it. She'll also give me my sister, who will be scared and want to sit on a low, bottom seat.

"Go ahead, scaredy cat," I say to her, "Sit down here." We've just given our money to Mr. Cantenegro and we are standing on a red metal grille at the base of the ride. Some kids are already strapped in above us.

"I'm going up there," I say to Mr. Cantenegro, pointing to the top. He smiles at me. I don't think he speaks English too well so smiling saves him energy. Then I point to a lower seat for Susie. He understands, and we all get strapped in.

Then he pulls a big lever, and the Tilt-a-Whirl starts rocking from side to side, like the pendulum on Grandma's clock. First gently, but I'm holding tight onto the bar across my lap because I know that soon it will be the exciting-like-you-might-get-killed part. Before you know it, everyone's screaming because you can't help it, like peeing, you'll explode if you keep it in. The whole world is racing and crazy. It's so un-boring that my stomach starts tilting into my mouth. My sister is pale and her mouth is open in a little O. I can't hear her voice because of all the noise of the engine and the other kids whooping, including Joey Fioretti who is having a blast even though his father is dead. You can forget everything but tilting and whirling. I mean that if Art Linkletter came here to interview me for television now and said, "What is your name?" I might say Houdini, or Marilyn Monroe; I could say anything now because I'm pretty out of my mind now.

Just when I think the whole world is a totally exciting place, I hear the engine start to slow down and the screaming die off, as if they were both from one source. My sister has her hand over her mouth, like she's going to throw up. Joey's head is thrown back like he just threw a Hershey's Kiss into the air and is trying to catch it in his mouth. Diane Benson's eyes are wide, like she just saw Frankenstein's monster.

Slower and slower we go until 79th Street looks like itself again. The apartment buildings are on the ground instead of in the air. Too bad. The grass isn't growing over the roof. Too bad. My sister looks like herself. Too bad. The engine putters down to nothing. I'm just me and everyone's just them. Mr. Cantenegro silently unlocks the lap bars and helps each of us down the metal steps, holding our elbows like we're old people. The ground feels like air for a few seconds when you first step down on it. Then it's the same old concrete.

Later in the afternoon, Mr. Stanley and his ice cream truck come back. This time my mother says I can buy an ice cream sandwich. It's a good, good day. I sit on the curb and lick and chew until it's gone. Then I lick all the chocolate sandwich stuff off my fingers and walk back toward Joey's house. Maybe we can play skellies again. Just as I look both ways before crossing the street, I see two dollar bills on the grass. I can't believe it, but there they are! I pick them up fast and run upstairs to tell my mother.

"Are you sure they don't belong to someone?" she asks. She's making salad for a change.

"I don't think so, they were just lying there, isn't it great? It's a miracle!"

"If they don't belong to someone else it's great," she says, "let's wait and see what happens."

What happens is that Amy, down the street, is even luckier than I am because she finds a five-dollar bill. Then Diane finds one single. We don't know where they came from, and no one comes to our door and asks for them back. All anyone says, if they're a kid, is "You're lucky!" All anyone says, if they're a grownup, is, "Are you sure it doesn't belong to someone else?" I wonder if Mr. Stanley lost them, but keep my idea to myself. "Two bucks," as my father calls it, is a lot of money, so I'll keep my Mr. Stanley idea to myself because even if it was him, it wasn't his money, it was the ice cream company's money and Good Humor is very rich because they have all these trucks filled with all this ice cream. Money is nice to have, for candy, comic books, and new clothing, and usually I have to work for it.

I have two regular jobs, which is good, because I like nice clothes and so I need the money. It means taking the subway to 34th Street in Manhattan to buy them, but it means saving up first, which means baby-sitting for the Mintons and for the Friedmans, my main customers. Each family has its problems—not *challenges* as my mother calls everything difficult, *problems*.

The Mintons are nice people who live only around the corner. They have two kids, Dave and Ellen. The kids are not the problem because they're usually fast asleep by the time I get there and they stay that way. Only once did Dave wake up and have to pee. It was a little embarrassing because I had to help him find his pee thing, which involved a lot of snapping and messing with complicated yellow Dr. Dentons. When we were finally in reach of it, I said, "Dave, you take over." And he did, with his eyes closed. When he was finished, I helped him snap it all up and watched him fall back into bed.

I never once saw Ellen awake in all the times I baby-sat because she's such a good sleeper, but what I did see awake were mice. My mother thinks it's because Mrs. Minton is a poor housekeeper. I think it might be because she leaves out such great food—candy, popcorn, chips—something my mother never, ever does because she thinks it's junk and not good for you.

When the Mintons leave ("We'll be back by midnight," they always say), I carry the junk to the couch and arrange the little bowls around me. Then I get my feet up off the floor and cover my legs with the blanket

Mrs. Minton leaves for me. I try to keep the blanket away from my face because of Minton germs as I watch TV and start falling asleep. That's when I always hear them, the mice I mean, scurrying all over the brown rug just as I'm dozing off. They are pretty ugly with gray ratty fur and skinny tails. I'd rather look at ants, so long as they're not the red kind, which once got into my shorts and made a dinner of my behind.

The Minton's couch is like a dirty boat, and the brown rug is like bad water. One night I'm baby-sitting and finally fall asleep. Then, before I know it, they're home. First I hear the key in the lock, then the sounds of them walking in. I look up at the clock on top of the side table and I'm always glad if it's late because that means I made money sleeping. Tonight it's 2:15. That's great! Mr. Minton always gives me the fifty cents for an extra hour even if I've slept only fifteen minutes into it.

It's strange putting your coat on in the middle of the night and going out half-asleep with a man who is not your father. It's shocking when it's winter and cold, but Mr. Minton is always considerate. He never tries to make conversation, just walks me right to my door, then watches as I open it with the key my mom gives me for these occasions.

It's too bad about the mice. I wonder if Mr. Minton thinks Mrs. Minton is a terrible housekeeper the way my mother does, or if he loves her too much to notice. Maybe he doesn't care about mice, or thinks they're cute. Maybe his own mother had mice, and he believes that mice and people living in the same house is normal. I wrote a little poem about it:

The Mintons have mice
and that isn't nice.

But they also have candy,
and that's pretty dandy.

The Friedmans have no mice, but they have a sleep-walker named Joanie. Mrs. Friedman warned me about this on the phone when she first asked me to baby-sit. She said, "Not to worry, she just walks around a little." But I did worry. The first time I baby-sat for Joanie and her little brother, Scott, I couldn't help looking from the TV down the dark hall that led to their bedroom and thinking of Lady Macbeth, who washed her hands all the time. I kept mixing up that kind of washing and Joanie's sleepwalking because both are pretty spooky when you think about it. I baby-sat three times and nothing happened, and I was beginning to wish Mrs. Friedman hadn't warned me because I wasted so much energy being nervous, but I guess she felt it was her responsibility to prepare me.

Finally it's the fourth time, and I'm just falling asleep when I hear the slow swishing of pajama feet on the wooden floor. Then there she is—Joanie. Her eyes are closed, but it's her. Same chubby little body and brown hair cut in a straight line at the top of her round shoulders. She begins walking into the living room saying things.

"What?" I ask her. I don't know if you're supposed to talk to sleepwalkers, but now I'm more interested than scared; I'm investigating, like Sherlock Holmes.

"What did you say, Joanie?" She's standing still and I've put a firm but gentle hand on her shoulder.

"*Shlam bewgusop,*" she says.

Maybe she speaks foreign languages in her sleep; maybe she's dreaming she's in India and knows the Indian language. If a French girl can walk into our junior high school with a beer in her lunchbox, then Joanie Friedman can definitely sleepwalk and speak Indian.

"How are you?" I ask. Nothing. She just stands there, her eyelids fluttering like two nervous butterflies.

"*Zinf alom*?" I ask. I just make it up.

She turns around and starts walking back to her bed, gets into it, and snorts like a little horse. I pull her blanket over her.

Joanie has definitely gone up in my estimation. She has proven that even though she lives in our really boring neighborhood, she is unique. Her sleepwalking proves that she has the potential to be an extraordinary individual.

"How did it go?" Mr. Friedman asks when they get home. He is very pale. My mother said it's because he has diabetes. The Friedmans are always home by midnight. Maybe it's because of the diabetes.

"Fine," I say. I don't tell them about Joanie. I don't want to ruin the great strangeness by talking about it. It's a quick trip home. I put my three dollars into an envelope in my dresser, then get undressed, into my pajamas, then into my own little nest, I mean bed.

°°°

I've noticed that everyone loves different things: Joanie loves sleepwalking, my mother loves making salad, Linda Solomon loves being grumpy, my sister loves having fits, Bonnie Solomon loves polishing shoes, God supposedly loves us all, and I love sitting on my bed and reading. But getting back to Bonnie Solomon, on Saturdays she's always got shoes all lined up on the landing outside the door to our garden apartment—grown-up shoes, girl shoes, boy shoes. I see her father's big brown oxfords. She's got lots of polish handy too—white, brown, red, black. And cloths, a separate one for each of the colors, which are set neatly beside the matching bottles. She's kneeling next to all this stuff and smiling, showing her big teeth.

"Do you want your shoes polished?" she pleads.

"Sure," I say, looking down at her, "I hate polishing shoes."

She looks at my brand-new sneakers, then up at me and says, "Well, go up and get them." At least she's smart enough to know that my new sneakers don't need polishing, what they need is dirtying.

"Okay." I turn around, open the big heavy door, and head up to the second floor to our apartment.

"Who is it?" my mom calls out.

"It's me." I get my brown penny loafers from my closet.

"See ya, Mom," I tell her. She's dusting the furniture for a change.

Bonnie reaches up for my loafers with two hands, like you'd reach for a baby, a cute one. Or for Johnny Mathis. Not how any normal person reaches for something like crummy shoes. The pennies in mine are scratched and dull, and the heels are worn out on the outsides because of how I walk.

"Here," I say to Bonnie, "have a great time." I'm being snotty. Maybe I'm a little jealous that she can have such a great time with a pair of shoes. "It's because she's simple," my mom says. Something about how when she was born, her head got stuck. It's much more complicated for me to be happy. It takes Michael Shulman meeting my eyes more times than Carol's or Barbara Cohen's. It takes a really good book, like *Gone With the Wind*. It takes accepting that sometimes I don't think God is so good and that's okay. Things like that because I'm not simple, I'm "sensitive," they say, and my father says I'm too sensitive, especially about criticism. "Genie hates criticism," he always says. But who in the world would like to hear, "You're not doing well enough in school," or, "We know you could do better because you have potential." Who would like to hear her mother say,

"Those sneakers look terrible with that dress...you should be wearing flats because that's what they wear."

"Who is 'they'?" I ask, and my mother looks back down at my sneakers, wrinkles up her nose, and shrugs.

Sometimes I think my parents are trying to do to me what Bonnie does to her shoes—make me perfect, shiny, and ideal. My mother really works at it—she will lick her finger and wipe some tiny dirt or something from my cheek, and although she's a very clean person, it smells disgusting. She's always fussing over what I wear too. "It's my body," I tell her.

"Teenagers need to express themselves, their individuality," I say and I can tell by the way she lowers her eyes she knows I'm right even though I'm not yet thirteen. I guess she can't help it because even if she manages to keep her mouth shut about my outfits, her eyes tell me something's wrong with me, especially if I'm wearing dark colors.

When I get back from my friend Carol's, maybe three hours later, Bonnie is finished. There are the perfectly matched pairs of shoes in perfect rows like married couples. She has them in a little semicircle for display.

"Genie!" she yells. I'm standing right next to her.

"Here," she says, and stands up. Her legs are like poles, her eyes are wild and excited, I mean the eyeballs move around.

"Great job, Bonnie," I say, "very nice." Then I go upstairs and put my perfect shoes in the shoe bag, one shoe into each little shoe pocket. They make a swishy sound against the plastic as they drop in. Then I look through my stack of books from the library and hope that one of them will be as exciting to me as my shoes were to Bonnie.

15

My mother closes the venetian blinds and leaves them that way. Maybe she thinks I'm dying, or that if I see the sky I might want to go outside. My temperature is high and I'm sweaty. I'm sick and I don't want to go out, I don't want to do anything. She comes in and puts a wet pink washcloth with a black "Z" on it on my forehead. She gives me aspirin and juice. She rushes in and out of my room a lot. I wish she'd just sit down and talk to me, but she's too busy. Maybe she's worried. I'm worried because she called the doctor three times and maybe I am dying, but the way I feel now, I don't care. It's like I weigh a ton, and night and day are the same really—just sleep, sleep, sleep. Maybe I'm dead already, I'm so hot. But I heard dead people get cold, so I guess I'm not.

Dr. Silverman is coming at 4 o'clock. My mother is cleaning my room and dusting the blinds so that a little light comes in. Maybe it will make me blind.

Dr. Silverman has a little mustache and a big black bag that opens so wide, you can't believe it. He wears a coat and tie, a fancy hat. My mother talks to him in the voice I hate—sweet, sweet, sweet. I think she wants the doctor to like her. If you want someone to like you though, it's not a good idea to try very hard because the person will know you're trying and wonder why, and also they might think that you're hiding the fact that you are mean underneath. "Be yourself," I'd say. Unless you really are basically mean; then, I'd say, "Act like a nice person." Most people are okay, Dr. Silverman is really okay. He has white clean hands that smell good.

He looks big to me, but that's because I'm lying down. He looks in my ears, presses my tongue with a big stick that makes me gag, looks in my eyes. I'm lucky because this time I don't have to get undressed.

I have the mumps, bad. He asks my mother all about my fever as if it were the World Series. She answers very seriously: 102, 103, etc. She has written all of this down on a pad of white paper, which she holds in her hand like the waiter at the Chinese restaurant when he takes our order.

The doctor leaves and then in a few days I start to feel better. It takes time because I'm so weak, but then, before you know it, I can go outside. Walking outside for the first time after a week in bed is like entering a brand-new world. It is so bright I can't believe it, maybe like the Garden of Eden. My legs feel a little empty and my chest too. "Be patient," my mother says, and she's right because in a few days I think I'm normal. But normal is different—normal is wonderful.

Then I find out that I'm not quite normal. I didn't even know it for a while, but I'd answer the phone and say, "No one's there" because I heard nothing. After Selma called and heard me do this twice, she said to my mother, "Something must be wrong with Genie's hearing." Mom tested it and whispered into my right ear. "You said, 'I love you'," I said. Then she whispered into the left. "Nothing," I said. She tried again. "Nothing," I said. I thought that the mumps made me deaf, but we went to an ear doctor in

Manhattan and he said it wasn't the mumps, but that Dr. Silverman gave me too much Aureomycin, which killed the nerve and that was that. I think it bothered Mom more than me. Things happen. I can hear if I turn my head the right way. When I lie down to go to sleep, I can put my good ear down on the pillow and it's very quiet. I could have had polio, or been retarded. I found myself consoling her. If God loves us the way my mother loves me, I bet He's pretty sad sometimes.

16

I have to go to Hebrew School after regular school on Mondays, Wednesdays and Fridays so I can learn to be a real Jew. Hebrew school is pretty boring, but I'm a kid and so I have no choice, which isn't fair. But to think of it, it's a lot better to be a Jewish kid than it is to be the other kind of kid, a baby goat, because then, according to the Bible, you can be sacrificed, which means burned (killed) because, for some reason, God likes the smell of burning meat. Me, I don't care for it at all, especially lamb chops, which have what my dad calls a "peculiar" odor because, for some peculiar reason, my dad likes the word peculiar and uses it whenever possible.

In Hebrew school we read the Bible story of Jacob, the son of Abraham, who was a pretty tricky character, although his mother, Rebecca, was even trickier than he was. Here's the thing: Abraham got really old, even older than my grandfather who is seventy. For some crazy reason, people in the Bible live over 100 years—maybe God liked people better back then because they hadn't been around long enough to make a lot of trouble like they did in World War I and World War II. Anyway, Abraham was something like 120, and he was dying. Now he had two kids, Jacob and

Esau, who were twins. Esau was red and hairy, and Jacob was more normal-looking and, like my sister and me, they didn't get along, but that's another story, "sibling rivalry." Well, because Abraham preferred Esau, he decided that he was going to give him all this stuff in his will. Back then it was things like land and animals because they didn't have stocks and bonds and houses and money. If I were him, I'd split it because that's fair. I think my dad likes my sister better than me, and my mom likes me better than my sister. I'd never say that, but I can tell; nevertheless (that's a long, good word), I know my dad and mom would be fair if they were dying because they try to be fair now: we have the same Formica desks with black wrought-iron legs, same beds and dressers and lamps, same spring and winter coats.

But, as I said, Rebecca wasn't fair and wanted Jacob to get all the stuff and since she was only about 100 and still hopping around while Abraham was 120 and probably really worn out lying in his bed in a tent somewhere, she (Rebecca) got Jacob to pretend he was Esau to trick him so Jacob would get all the goats and land. Well, the Bible, I must say, is even stranger than Grimm's fairy tales, which are pretty strange. Rebecca gets these animal skins and puts them on Jacob's body, kind of like the mink stole my mother wears when she goes out on Saturday nights. Wearing animals is pretty terrible. What if some bear decided it wanted to wear your skin? Anyway, Jacob looks and feels really hairy and Abraham is tricked into giving him all his stuff. Poor Esau, he really lost out. Like some of the contestants on *The $64,000 Question* show on TV who lose tons of money because they don't remember some dumb fact like Ponce de Leon was looking for the Fountain of Youth. I think being young isn't so great, so why waste your time looking for youth? But that's another story too.

Anyway, Esau must have suffered a lot and there are lots of wars in the Bible after that because he was cheated. When someone is cheated, it leads to trouble, it's just human nature. Things can be going great, like you're getting an A in French and then you're taking a dictation test and Mademoiselle Delson says "Paris" and you listen hard and write "Parie." Then you stare at the page and know it's wrong, but P-A-R-I-S just doesn't look like "Parie," which is what she said, and so you get a B, not an A, on your test.

°°°

It seems to me that in the Bible fathers were a lot more powerful than they are now when they just go to work, carry out the garbage, nod to the mothers, and fall asleep over their newspapers after supper. God, who was the first father, was all-powerful and in the Bible it says that in the beginning, He created the world. He looked upon the nothingness, which is really hard to imagine, I mean how can you look at nothing, but He's God and so He did, and then He said, "Let there be light!" and the darkness moved away and there was half dark and half light, the first day, and God said that it was good. Then He made sky on top and dry stuff on the bottom, and separated waters for oceans from land and then created trees and fruits and vegetables, including lima beans, which are awful, and flowers, which are great. God said all of this was good too. He was very pleased with Himself, and I can't blame Him for that. I'd be pretty proud too if I could do such things. I can hardly paint a good picture of land and sky with only one tree, it's all out of perspective and babyish looking, but I'm pretty good at poetry and stickball.

So, to make a long story short, I don't have too much trouble believing the creation story and the idea that all those new, amazing things were good in God's eyes, but I do have some problems with the idea that God is always and forever a " He," kind of a bigger-than-life man. "It takes two to tango," as they say, and if God is so great, greater than anything, then God has to be more than just a "He," although I don't know what the right word for this "more" would be.

Part of my confusion, or skepticism as my father calls questioning things most people take for granted, like the importance of money, lawyers, doctors and, especially, politicians, is that most of the men I see around, except for the president of the United States and my father's friend Philly, who is a fabulous double-talker, are pretty quiet. They don't go around saying, "Let there be…" or "This is good!" and I really don't see the things they create. I know they make money, but all I really see of that is the fifty cents in my hand which I get for allowance each week. The mothers are the ones who really make things—tuna casseroles, tidy beds, embroidered tablecloths, etc.

The Bible says that God created man in His own image, "in the image of God created He Him," and that Eve, the first woman, came out of a rib in Adam's chest. I just can't imagine that. First of all, a mother is the one who creates you because she grows you inside her and then gives birth to you. I'm not so dumb that I don't know some of the facts of life, including the fact that the man has to put the sperm/seed inside the woman. But putting a seed in something is nothing compared to making it grow and then pushing it out.

My friend Ellen and I once snuck into the Astoria Theatre to see a movie called *Thank You Dr. Lamaze*. He was a French doctor and the movie showed a real mother giving birth to a real baby, blood and all. Now that's what I call work, panting like mad and pushing out a new life, trying to get this big head out a small opening. I lied and told my mother that I saw *Seven Brides for Seven Brothers*, which I did see the next Saturday.

After seeing the birth in the movie, it seemed even more logical that a woman or a combination woman/man would be the creator of things like heaven and earth, and day and night, and that men were more likely to wash cars, pay bills, and fall asleep reading newspapers.

To be fair about it, I really don't know what God is, no one really does, but I think my idea of God as a combination of a man and a woman is a pretty good one. I know I'm just a plain girl with an active imagination, but I think that if God were a He who managed all this creation, He'd need someone to feed Him, make his bed, fold his wash, etc. Maybe it's because my mother is so much more the boss of our house than my father that my perspective is off. My mother says, "Carl, carve the turkey please" or "Carl, please take out the garbage," and off he goes. So it's hard to read the Bible and believe it's true based on what I see in the world of our apartment and neighborhood. But big things and little things are related. For example, you see a tree in the springtime and the leaves are tiny but shaped as they are supposed to be—different for a maple or a birch—but, in any case, the little leaf becomes a bigger one with the same design and so it must be with God and people...I mean little things and bigger ones are really versions of the same thing. So maybe people are smaller versions of God. And since people are male and female, it makes sense that God must be both too.

ooo

Besides reading the Bible in Hebrew school, we learn to read Hebrew, and these funny, squiggly shapes in the prayer book begin making sense. Sort of. What I mean is I learn how to say words, to sound them out, but I don't know what most of them mean. To think about it, that actually fits in with most things in my life, I mean I learn what to say, but not what things really mean, and that's what I want to learn.

Sometimes I think I'd do better living in a fairy tale where things may be strange, like sleeping for 100 years, but end up making some kind of sense. Maybe when I'm older, life will make sense, but for now, back to the synagogue for the high holy days. Many Jewish people go on these days only: Rosh Hashanah, the New Year, and Yom Kippur, the Day of Atonement. Yom Kippur is the holiday that has really begun to bother me because I have to stand in a pew, make a fist, hit my chest, and ask to be forgiven for all the sins I have committed that year: "For the sin that we have sinned before You in a session of vice; for the sin we have sinned before You through impure lips," just to name a couple. It makes me angry to beg forgiveness because the truth is that I'm always trying to be good. I guess it's psychological—I want my mom and dad to love me and they seem to do the job better when I do what they want. So I'm good, good, good and so what's this deal about sin? And here I am standing in synagogue hitting myself (softly) and worrying about being inscribed in the Book of Life for another year because of some sin I have no idea about and I'm all of twelve and a half years old. Why should a basically good girl like me have to be afraid of God? It says in the Bible that the fear of the Lord is the beginning of wisdom. I don't get it. Your parents make you, and love you because you are theirs, so if God made us, why doesn't He just love us because we are His? Why do we have to beat our chests and keep apologizing?

In spite of all this, I like being Jewish. The little things about it—the food and hugging. Also, we talk more and seem to have more fun than the Christians I know, who are so serious, like our neighbors, the Gilmans. They once invited me to dinner and it was very formal and quiet. At the end of the meal, which was bland (but not burned), Mrs. Gilman complimented me on how I used my napkin to wipe my lips. "Genie is very polite," she said to her daughter, Elaine, "you should use your napkin as frequently as she uses hers." The truth is I was putting on a good show, using manners I've seen in movies where people are richer and more polite than we really are at my house.

When I don't like being Jewish is when it is Christmas, and you see once again that Santa isn't interested in you. He's never bothered to learn your address, which is 22-29 79th Street in Queens near La Guardia Airport. Maybe he doesn't like airplanes, I thought when I was little, maybe he's afraid they'll hit his sled or the noise will scare Rudolph or something. I'm not sure. But I do know that I don't matter to him one tiny bit.

In school the windows are pasted with snowflakes and with colored paper cut into the shape of bells. Red and green ribbons are everywhere. Most of the kids are really excited. George Insana drums the heel of his shoe even harder and faster than usual in the last row of class. He drums it so fast now it's a blur. But Arnold, who is Jewish like me, slowly pulls some used gum from under his desk and makes disgusting long and sticky strings of it. Maybe he feels left out too.

A few weeks before Christmas is our Chanukah. My mother takes the silver menorah out and the candles and tries to make a really big fuss. She calls Susie and me to come watch her light the candles. It's the same fake voice she used when we went on our trip to Canada and she kept saying, "Isn't that beautiful?" If a grownup says something over and over, do you know what happens? You start to think the opposite. My mom keeps saying Chanukah is just as important as Christmas. Sure!

We do get Chanukah presents, and we get one each night for eight nights because that's how long this little amount of oil burned and it was a miracle. On the first night, I get a really good present, like a sweater. But on some of the other nights, especially nights number six, seven, or eight, I get a paint set, or jacks...what's so great about that? Also, we know what we're getting ahead of time because we sneak into the big bottom drawer of Mom's dresser and push away her bras and panties and look at the presents before she wraps them.

ooo

In school we begin singing Christmas songs like, "You better not pout, you better not cry, you better not...I'm telling you why, etc."

I always feel like everyone forgot me when we sing this. I know no Santa is watching me, making no list, checking it not even once. I know that another man, but not fat, and dressed different from this Santa, checked on us a lot and he didn't like what he saw. His name was Hitler and he had a mustache and he killed a lot of Jewish people and put numbers on their arms. My mother says we are "chosen" and special. This doesn't always seem to be a good thing.

In school we keep practicing *Noel* and *Deck the Halls* and *O Little Town of Bethlehem*. We stand in line in size place and sing while Miss Marsh crisscrosses her arms in the air. She stands on top of a wooden milk box to make her taller and I'm afraid she'll fall off.

The real problem is *O Come All Ye Faithful* because at the end of it you have to say these words which, if you sing them and you're Jewish, it's a sin. My mother thinks it's such a sin that she tells me, "Just move your lips as if you were saying the words, but be careful not to ever say them." Once though, after we practiced this song three times in a row, I was so tired that I forgot and sang, "Christ, Our Lord."

Thank God nothing happened, I was scared it would—like a bolt of lightning would hit me, or I'd have a heart attack. The next week I lost my wallet and maybe that had to do with saying the words, but I'm always losing things anyway.

After Christmas is over, my mother goes to talk to our principal, Miss Shannon, and says something about the carols and probably about other things because my mother has ideas, lots of them. Then Miss Shannon calls me to her office and says that I don't have to sing *O Come All Ye Faithful* ever again and pats me on the head. The following Christmas Miss Marsh even teaches us a Chanukah song, but Arnold Rosenberg and I are the only ones who know it and besides, it's a pretty stupid song and doesn't have a good tune like *Noel.*

I think that Chanukah is like a hand-me-down dress from someone with blue eyes and blond hair. She just gave this holiday to me without knowing who I am—me, the girl who once saved up all the money she needed for pink toe shoes, me, the one who keeps trying to figure out right from wrong and who knows that white and Negro people are really the same.

The Chanukah oil is just not such a good idea. Oil in a lamp is not nearly as great as a baby born in a barn with animals and men dressed up in jewelry with crowns and great presents that smell like frank-incense. But I'd never be invited to go a party in that barn, that's just how it is.

ooo

Being Jewish at Halloween is not a problem. I really, really like Halloween. A lot of it is that I get to eat tons of candy. My mother doesn't believe in eating sugar.She thinks it's bad for you, and so when the neighborhood kids, David Minton, Bonnie and Linda Soloman, etc. have ice cream and cookies for dessert, what do we have? Fruit! I don't even like fruit. Maybe it is good for you, but so what? The kids who eat sugar look just as good as I do, and better than my sister, who is sick a lot with asthma even though she eats fruit for dessert. Anyway, when it's Halloween, we both get to go absolutely overboard on candy for about a week.

When I was younger, this is how it happened. First of all, Mom takes me to Woolworth's to buy a costume, and if I'm lucky, it won't rip when I put it on, and it won't fit next year so I can get a different one then. One year I got a gypsy costume—shiny blue for the skirt and yellow with little silver circles for the top, and also a little crown with red ties attached to it in order to keep it on your head. It's cute and I think some of the girls in my class will be wearing the same one, but I don't care. I like feeling like a different person for Halloween because I'm so used to feeling like myself all the time. The costume doesn't really make me a princess, but I feel like one anyway, a gypsy-princess.

My mom gives me a big brown bag from the supermarket for one hand and an orange and black box in the other. I'm the only kid with two hands full because I have to collect for UNICEF, a charity for poor children. Oh well. I don't really mind except it's hard to manage it all at once because my crown keeps slipping over my eyes and then I have to put down either my UNICEF box, or my paper bag in order to fix it so I can see where I'm going next. It's also hard to see because it's dark.

Bonnie, Linda, Susie, and I go in a pack. Susie is a ghost with a little sheet with holes for eyes over her head, and Linda is a pirate with a black patch over one of her eyes. Bonnie is wearing one of her mother's old dresses and keeps tripping over the hem. I try to help her by stuffing the dress under her belt, but then she steps on it again and we're back to square one.

"Bonnie," I tell her, after I've put down my box or bag for the millionth time, "next year you need a real Woolworth's costume so it's short enough for a kid."

She smiles and says okay, but I know she'll forget and I should tell Selma, her mother, but then I remember that grown-ups don't like you to tell them what to do—they only like to tell you what to do. Maybe it's because they got so sick of being told what to do when they were little that now, when they're big, they can't help being bossy.

Another reason Halloween is great is because you don't know who is who in your neighborhood. I always know who is who and it's always the same person doing the same things. But these three kids—one with a sheet, and two wearing everything black and masks, I don't really know who they are at all. I could guess, but I won't because the mystery part is better than being smart. I know they're boys and they're probably Joey Fioretti and Arnold

Rosenberg and Michael Shulman, but I'm going to pretend that they aren't those boys at all when they go by running and yelling, *h-o-o-o, h-o-o-o, h-o-o-o*, their shopping bags flying behind them. I'll watch and pretend they are real cowboys, or soldiers or detectives.

I love how the dark is like a big closet, not a really scary one, maybe just a little scary, and it's as if everyone has grabbed something crazy off a hanger and changed the world. In this new world, everyone speaks the same language, which is "Trick or Treat." And all the grown-ups are nice and generous with candy and smiles and "Wow, look at you" and "Oh, how pretty you are," and then they give you sweets and you hear the nice plop of a little chocolate bar hitting the other stuff.

On Halloween it's as if our whole neighborhood is like the game Candyland, but real, and the doors aren't locked and the windows are open and you don't have to draw a card or throw the dice to go anywhere. Everyone is happy.

This year Mr. Dubin gave me a whole dime. I thought of putting it into the UNICEF box, but changed my mind. He gave it to me. If he wanted to put it into the UNICEF box he could have. Instead, he opened his hand, showed me the shiny dime and dropped it into my bag. Then he did the same for the other girls. He is a nice man. I wonder why adults can't be like him more often. It seems they're always so busy trying to get money or keeping the house clean that they don't take time for fun…like Mr. Dubin showing me the little dime before throwing it in.

There is one exception—my dad's friend Philly who, as I mentioned, does take time for fun by talking double-talk, which is definitely not useful. He always has time for that. "Atta girl," he'll say, "how's it going *jing-amoon-vram-*

lakasham." Something like that. He's really good at this because just when I think I know exactly what he's saying, and it's normal, he says something like, "*Blamaroupoum*" in the middle of a regular sentence and I get all mixed up. He gets a real kick out of confusing people; I can tell he loves it when I look up at him and say, "What?!" Confusing people is a little mean.

After we're finished trick-or-treating, we go back home. Susie and I sit and spill our candies and money all over our beds, which are very close to each other because we share a room. I put all the pennies and my one shiny dime in one pile, then I shovel all the candies into another pile. It's great to see them all together and to know for sure that there's really a lot of good stuff this year, mainly chocolate. Susie wants to trade Necco wafers for a Nestle's Crisp, but I say, "No way, José." She says it's not fair because I got more good stuff than she did. I say," Life is not fair," which is one of the things my father says, and I say it just the way he does, staring down my imaginary glasses and emphasizing the "not" part. This makes her even madder, which I like. She counts out her chocolates and she has nine. I count mine and get seventeen. I tell her, "You know sweets aren't really good for you," but I slip her two Hershey's.

ooo

One Jewish holiday I really like is Passover, or Pesach, as my mother and grandparents call it. On Pesach my grandfather really looks like God because he's in a long white robe and sits at the head of the table surrounded by fluffy white pillows, like angel wings, which he leans back on like a King. The table is covered with food and sacred objects, including a blue velvet pouch with gold fringes, which holds three pieces of matzoh. There's a big silver goblet, polished by Grandma, with deep red Manischewitz poured into it for Elijah, the prophet who is supposed to visit. How he visits every Jewish house in the world, no less in this neighborhood, is beyond me, but we open the door for him every year.

There is also a fancy seder plate on the table with special spots for salt water to represent tears, *chaoroses* for mortar, a bone for something, a boiled egg for life, parsley, also for life, and bitter herbs for bitterness because we were slaves unto Pharaoh until God, in His mercy, delivered us by doing these terrible things to the Egyptians, like sending down hail, and giving them boils, and filling their fields with giant insects called locusts and most terrible of all, killing their first born. I'm sorry, but I think he went too far with that one. Can you imagine killing a baby?

We eat a lot of great food—chicken soup with matzoh balls, gefilte fish with horseradish, and so forth. But all of that is not as great as getting to drink wine, which makes all of us a bit cuckoo, and so we laugh a lot and even my agnostic father looks happy. We all do because, in fact, we are happy, maybe because of the Manischewitz, which you're supposed to drink four cups of. Even my grandfather, Menachem Mendel Greenberg, is smiling.

On a more serious note, I love the story of Passover, the Haggadah we read aloud from by going around the table and taking turns. I like the idea of freedom; it's a very important concept. No one should be a slave to another, we are all part of creation and celebrating freedom every year with your family is something I wish all people, slaves and sick people, crazy and normal ones, would do. I love how everyone's voice is different, each with its own tone and rhythm, I love how every spring the words we say are the same from the same wine-stained little Manischewitz booklets while outside the trees are making little leaves and the grass is popping up.

I wish we'd read aloud together more often, especially from the big book by the poet Walt Whitman called "Leaves of Grass," which has a green rough cover that is woven. Walt Whitman says things I like a lot, such as:

And I know that the spirit of
God is the brother of my own,
And that all the men ever born are also my brothers,
and the women my sisters and lovers....

But like all amazing, hard-to-understand things, I have to think about his poems alone. Funny though, when I do, with the afternoon light coming into my room softly, I feel something wonderful inside me, and maybe that's God.

18

My mother has ideas about everything, and for her, everything is either good or bad. Good is: 1. Clean—furniture, windows, dishes, my teeth, my clothing, my mouth. The second time I told her to shut up (I don't remember why), she put a bar of yellow/orange Dial soap in my mouth to clean it out. It was awful. 2. Neat—the table set right, my clothes folded in the drawers, the bed made and the bedspread smoothed so that it's not wrinkled one bit and the pillows on the couch puffed up and don't put your head on the couch because of hair oil. "What hair oil?" I ask her, touching my hair and looking at my fingertips. "Oil", she says, "oil." In the Bible it says, "God will anoint they head with oil," like it's a blessing. But to my mother it is a curse.

Bad is: 1. Toenail clippings in the sink, thumb sucking or nail biting, nasty words like shut up, not coming for supper when called, not cleaning your plate, which means eating everything off it nicely with a fork, finishing it whether you like it or not because of the starving children in India, then wiping your mouth with a napkin.

°°°

"Who cares?" I think when my mother complains that the tablecloth always gets dirty during dinner. I'm helping her put it on before we eat. I have two corners in my hands, and she's got the other ends. We flip it up and let it fall, same as we do with sheets. What does she expect from a tablecloth? "Cleanliness is next to godliness," she says. What about storms that get things really dirty and disorganized? What about lint or dust? She thinks dust is dirty, and yet it is what our bodies are said to return to.

°°°

Every week it is the same thing for meals: Monday night is meatloaf, Tuesday night is dairy (which usually means tunafish casserole), Wednesday night is liver (because it's good for you), Thursday night is hamburger, Friday night is chicken, Saturday is leftovers, and Sunday is eating out, either at a Chinese restaurant or at my grandparents'. I wonder why it is always the same. "Easier," my mother says as she tries to pry the blackened string beans from off the bottom of the pot. She *always* burns the string beans, and other things.

At home, Mom sits at one end of the table, Dad on the other and Susie and I are across from each other. Bad idea. It's liver, so you know already it's Wednesday, the worst night of the week for eating. It's also always very boring at the dinner table. I hate liver, even with lots of onions. "It's good for you," my mother says for the millionth time when I begin to make faces at my plate, "it has lots of iron."

My father is sort of still at work, I mean I can tell he's thinking about work or something else. I can see him chewing his food to my right. Maybe he's just "out to lunch," which is what he says about me when I don't answer anyone because I'm reading. Even our new parakeet, Lassie, looks bored sitting on her little swing staring at us. The light coming in through the blinds is a dull gold, as it is in fall, but it's spring. Is this life? When I can't stand it anymore, I kick Susie under the table. I have a way of reaching her by leaning to one side and swinging at a special angle. It always works.

"Genie kicked me!" she yells.

Then there's a long, heavy silence. My mother stares at her plate and my father, as usual, says nothing. So I do it again. Susie yells louder. My mother begins to look seriously at my father, but all she can see now is the top of his head with only a little hair on it because he's getting pretty bald and now he's looking down at his plate. My mother will have to say something because she thinks it's her duty as a mom.

"Stop it girls!" she says placing her fork down diagonally on her plate.

But I don't stop, I keep at it. Susie too. She yells louder and stands up. I glance at the untouched liver on her plate, which looks like bloody leather. She runs from the table to the bathroom and locks the door behind her with a huge slam. Same as always.

What happens next is that my mother nods at my father. Then he gets up, opens the front drawer of the breakfront and takes out a screwdriver. Susie keeps yelling, but it sounds like she has a towel in her mouth because she's behind the closed bathroom door. My father sticks the screwdriver into a little hole in the doorknob and forces the door open. Even though Susie locks it from inside, he can open it from the outside. Then my father slowly pulls her toward the table, nicely holding her hand, and she sits down. She's quiet now, but she twitches her shoulders back and forth every few seconds so we remember she is still emotional, like the famous actress, Sarah Bernhardt.

What my father does to my sister is a heck of a lot nicer than what Abraham did to Isaac. Abraham thought that God wanted him to sacrifice his only son, a cute little boy; he thought he heard some holy voice command him to do it. So, like he was a kid in school, not one of the big shots of the whole Jewish religion, he takes his son to the mountain like he's taking him to a baseball game, and just as he's about to chop the poor kid's head off, an angel stops his hand and he gets a big reward. As if the kid were a fish or a cow. Why would God demand such a thing? I don't get it. I should have been born a boy in Europe long ago, the kind with *payes* who studies all day long and debates the fine points of the Torah. I'd have fun with that, and could ask all my questions, but the hairdo would be a definite problem what with those long curls getting into your eyes and mouth.

But returning to our house and its problems...my mother writes to *The New York Post* psychologist, Dr. Rose Franzblau. She writes, "Dear Dr. Franzblau...." Then she describes the dinner table (but leaves out the burned string beans and liver, which I don't think is fair). Dr. Rose Franzblau answers and I can't believe it— but there it is in *The New York Post*, we're famous. My mother signs the letter "Mr. and Mrs. Upset in Queens."

First I think this Doctor Franzblau is not stupid. She says my parents need to talk to Susie and me, to get us "involved" so we enjoy family time at the table. Later, when I think more about it, I decide that she is stupid. Because it's too late. The way we eat is a habit, like sucking my thumb, which I tried to stop for so long before I could. But my parents try. The next night, my dad says, "How was school, Genie?" Wow, I think. Hmmmm. "Fine," I say.

I wonder if my parents talk to each other in bed because they don't do much of it in front of us. But there is dancing in our house. Maybe because they're really glad to be done sitting at the table eating the same foods night after night. Anyway, my mother and father tango, then they do the foxtrot to Sinatra. Next Mom and I do the twist to the Chubby Checker album, and the floor bounces up and down a little and the saucers and plates in the breakfront rattle and clatter.

19

It's like the exodus in the Bible—a lot of the mothers and fathers in our neighborhood are all going to a fancy hotel in the Catskill Mountains where there's lots of food, swimming pools, and other stuff. I'm not interested, but my mother certainly is. She's packing her shiniest dress and black high heels; she's packing her red v-neck sweater, her shorts, her fake diamond earrings, and two necklaces, a silver one with a green big heart on it and a gold one with pearls in a circle.

"I'm not going," I say when she asks if I want to go.

"You can socialize there, you can dance with the boys, maybe Walter." Walter Mandell?! He has greasy hair and I think he has a crush on me because he's always looking at me, but I'm never really sure on account of his crossed eyes. Plus he wears thick glasses. "No thanks," I say.

That night my mother and father have one of their powwows at the dinner table. I can tell it's an important one because my mother licks her fork, puts it down diagonally on her plate, crosses her arms, rests on her elbows, leans forward, blinks, looks up at my dad and says, "Carl, we need to have a discussion..."

I eat faster and try not to look up. My sister, on the

other hand, imitates my mother's fork and arm motion, rests on her elbow, but rather than looking at our father, she looks up at the ceiling and begins batting her eyelids. This is another example of Sarah Bernhardt behavior. My mother ignores her.

"Genie doesn't want to go to the Concord with us."

My father shrugs his shoulders; he's not a Sarah Bernhardt sort of person at all. Susie says, "Then I'm not going." This surprises me, but I know she always has her own reasons for things, like maybe she 's afraid she'll get lost in the hotel lobby because it's so big, or maybe she'll get asthma because the swimming pool is cold....

"Well," continues my mother, "I've been thinking of asking Toby and Harry to take the girls for the weekend." (Toby, whose real name is Dorothy, is my aunt; Harry, whose real name is Max, is my uncle). This is when Susie throws her fork on the floor and whispers in a loud voice, "Never, never, never!" She doesn't look at anyone, just at her plate. My mother *tells her to pick up her fork immediately young lady*, then starts nagging her to eat. My mother reminds her again about the starving children in India. My sister is really skinny.

ooo

Two weeks later, the mothers and fathers leave without too much fuss and Susie and I are dropped off at Aunt Toby and Uncle Harry's house where cousins Ira and Robert live too.

When Cousin Robert was little, he used to sit in his playpen on the terrace and throw 78 records at us, but he's better—now he just runs around the living room yelling. Sometimes I try to calm him down because I'm older and I feel sorry for my aunt because of the noise. I get on my knees and hold him by his shoulders. I can feel his fast breathing on my face as I try to look into his little eyes, but it's like trying to look straight into a shooting star. He squirms out of my hands and runs again. Poor Aunt Toby—she has no idea what to do with him, so she vacuums the rugs all day. Maybe it's because the vacuum cleaner is louder than cousin Robert. In between cleanings, she stoops down to pick up the tiniest pieces of dirt, shmutz, that only she can see. It seems like she's bending over all the time, like Ruth and Naomi in the cornfields in the Bible.

On Sunday, everyone is happy because we're getting out of the house to drive to Grandma and Grandpa's apartment in Brooklyn. Uncle Harry is driving my dad's car because he doesn't have one of his own. My parents loaned him ours for the weekend; they got a ride with Selma and Dave, our neighbors.

"You'll enjoy it, Max," my father says to Uncle Harry. "Enjoy!" he commands as he breezes out the door after kissing Susie and me. This "Enjoy!" command is really dumb because telling people to enjoy something doesn't make them enjoy anything.

Once we're on the road, I discover a problem, a big one—Uncle Harry does not know how to drive. I'm surprised because I thought all grown-ups knew how to drive. Not him. He is sitting up front with Aunt Toby and Cousin Robert, who is so amazed that his father is behind the wheel that he's quiet for once. Susie, Ira, and I are in the backseat. Uncle Harry gets the car started and then the problems begin. They live on a hill in a town appropriately called Forest Hills, and every time Uncle Harry tries to move the car up this hill, it shakes like mad, then stops. He starts it again, then it shakes and dies. Uncle Harry is getting redder than usual (he's always a little red), and his cheeks are puffed out like a frog's. I am afraid he will have a heart attack. Aunt Toby is quiet, stiff, and white. Robert continues to sit still. In the backseat, Susie and I are giving each other looks; we know how a car is supposed to work, and this is not how. Uncle Harry finally gets us up the hill to the boulevard, but then it gets even worse because now he's going the wrong way down a one-way street. I know because all the other cars are coming at us and honking. One man in a hat sticks his head out of the window of his black Cadillac and yells. Uncle Harry is now red as a tomato, but he keeps going the wrong way because what else can he do? Finally, he makes a big circle by going the wrong way down three streets, and we're back where we started.

I am sweating in my brown coat. Sarah Bernhardt is too upset to even make a sound; she is squeezing her patent-leather pocketbook, which looks wet. Our cousin Ira keeps staring out the window. I consider thanking God for my father because he is a good driver, and thanking Him also for helping Uncle Harry with the car. We are now at the bottom of their hill. I don't mind the long walk up at all. I don't mind that my sister is holding my hand. The world looks pretty good—Cousin Robert is quietly holding Aunt Toby's hand, Uncle Harry is slowly walking with Ira at his side. We'll play cards this afternoon—War, or Rummy.

20

We never got to Grandpa's that day, but he and Grandma came to ours a few weeks later and my mother asked me to walk with Grandpa to Mr. Chessler's to buy the newspaper. What happened was that when we got to the corner of Ditmars and 79th he started running away from me yelling, "*Shikse, shikse!*" which is the name for a girl who is not Jewish. I ran after him, and then Mr. Flaum, our neighbor who always stands in front of his house smoking, ran with us. He's a gossip, but that day I was glad he was watching all the neighbors in order to find something to talk about. He caught up with Grandpa, put his arm around him, and said some nice things that calmed him down so he would walk home with us like a normal person.

After that, we kept visiting his and Grandma's house as usual, but things were not as usual. Sometimes he'd be sweet and quiet, his white yarmulke on top of his head as he moved his papers around in neat piles on top of the big dining room table, but other times he'd shake his big black prayer book in the air, yelling things.

ooo

We never yell in our house. My mother and father never raise their voices, only my sister and I have fights, but they are usually kicking under the dining room table kind of fights. Sometimes Susie yells, but then she runs to the bathroom and slams the door. Once my parents really did yell, and we ran into the hallway and whispered, DIVORCE, but they stopped.

°°°

The older Grandpa got, the angrier he became and I couldn't figure out why because he'd always been so nice. He owned a big drugstore and helped people by giving them apples or selling them powders and pills. He was kind to poor people, giving them medicine even if they didn't have money for it. Everyone liked him in his white coat with a high collar and his round eyeglasses that made him look like a rabbi. He talked softly and comforted people who were sick. What was he so angry about? I kept thinking about how God, too, got angry a lot and I couldn't fall asleep. I ended up having to turn my foam rubber pillow over and over for coolness.

When Grandpa died, I laughed, I couldn't help it. Dad got the call from Mom who was at the hospital with bars on the window called Credemore, then he put the receiver down and told us and I immediately cracked up. Then Susie started giggling too. After a while, I thought of my mother at the terrible place where Grandpa was, the one near the highway, and I stopped laughing. What would she be like now? Would she cry a lot? I never saw her cry except when Rin Tin Tin, the last parakeet we had, died and she held him in her lap wrapped in tissues. What did dying do to people anyway? Who would sit in their chairs? Grandpa had a beautiful dark wood chair with a high back for a king. Who would say his prayers? Grandpa prayed a lot. What would happen to Grandpa's books and papers and to his clothing, and what about his shoes? Then I began worrying about my teeth.

21

Because I sucked my thumb so much when I was little, my teeth stick out. They don't stick out so far that the kids tease me like they do Marlene Drexler—hers are like the wax ones some kids wear on Halloween to look like Dracula.

I should have stopped thumb sucking when I was a lot younger—that's what Dr. Ross, the orthodontist, reports. What I want to say (but don't) after he says this to me and my mother is, "I didn't want to stop then, I liked it, and besides it's none of your business." It feels good to make a little dark tent with your own hands over your own mouth and nose and put your thumb in. Now, it is true that thumb sucking is babyish and a little disgusting, but I hardly sucked it, I just kept it there like an arm or leg under a blanket. And I never hurt anyone doing this, except maybe my teeth.

Grown-ups have all these ideas about what you can do and when you can do it. For example, when I turned twelve, I was allowed to stay up until nine. It seems that God rules parents, or tries to, and parents rule kids, or try to. Rules, rules, rules....

The braces cost six hundred dollars, but my parents don't mind. My mother even seems a little proud about the whole thing. Maybe she was ashamed of how I looked before my teeth were straightened.. I'm not sure. She's always telling me how pretty I am, but as I said, I've noticed that sometimes when grown-ups say things over and over it's because they're thinking the opposite. For example, as I mentioned, my neighbor, Bonnie Sussman, is dumb. She can't answer easy math or think very well. Like if you say, "Do you want to go to Chessler's?" She'll look at you like you just asked her "The 64 Million-Dollar Question." Also, as I mentioned, she likes to polish shoes for about three hours straight. Anyway, I notice that when my mother walks out of our building and Bonnie is surrounded by the neighbors' shoes, my mother always stops and says, "Bonnie, you're so good at polishing shoes, you're doing such a fine job," and she bends down and picks one up and turns it around examining it, like it's gold or something. The point is that my mother knows Bonnie is slow and so she goes out of her way to be nice and she covers it up. And in covering it up she uncovers it.

But no one can cover up the fact that I need braces and so there I am. Dr. Ross's office is in a big building near the BMT elevated train and as I'm sitting in his fancy green leather seat with my mouth wide open, I see the trains through the blinds and hear the terrible noises they make. Dr. Ross shoves caps on my teeth, twists wires around them and sometimes takes impressions, which are shapes of your teeth pressed into some strange goopy stuff in trays that makes you feel like you're going to throw up.

Every time we visit his office and he tells my mother how well it's going, how fast my teeth are moving to where they should be, I feel kind of proud of them, my teeth, like they're really cooperative kids standing together nicely in a row.

Head gear, however, is a problem. Especially if you go

to summer camp, which I do, because other people besides your family members get to see you looking like a Martian with a big metal contraption in your mouth, and a peculiar cap with straps all over your head. It's terrible, far more embarrassing than buck teeth.

"Suffer for beauty," Bonnie and Linda's mother keeps preaching, just like she did when I complained about sleeping on rollers. She repeats this when I try to say good night to her and I can barely open my mouth to talk because of head gear. Do you really have to suffer for beauty? My parakeet is beautiful, the sky is beautiful and the painting my mother has of a ballet dancer by Toulouse-Lautrec with her skirt all twirled around her is beautiful too, and none of these things seem to be suffering.

22

As my teeth continue to straighten out, my dancing really doesn't and so Fara Lynn's Dance Studio is never my kind of place. There are mirrors on every wall, and there are barres in front of every mirror. I really don't like to watch myself—I'm not a bad dancer, but I'm also not that good. That's how I look too—just okay.

You should see Fara Lynn—she's old and very short, but she's really a great dancer. Her hair is yellowish red in a braid wound up on top of her head like a snake. She wears pink tights and her veins stick out under them so that it looks like there are baby snakes on her legs. "Fara Snake Lynn," I think. She has an accent, but my father says it's fake. My father likes to say everything is fake. My father thinks that doctors are fake, and politicians are my father's favorite fake. Besides "peculiar," "fake" is my father's favorite word. My mother calls this "cynical."

Fara Lynn is bossy, but I guess it's part of her job. She likes the best dancers the most, the ones who have toe shoes, and she always pays the most attention to them. I've noticed you can tell a lot about what people care about by what they look at. Fara Lynn does not look at me. I have to look at her though in order to copy her plié, assemblé, jété, pas de bourée.

The worst part of dancing school is always "across the floor." We line up in threes and of course Elise Lapinski and Diane Schecter are in the first row. I always head for the last. The problem with across the floor is that when it's your turn, suddenly the floor is a whole block long, with all this air and space you have to get across and it's always shocking that the room has grown so much. And you always think everyone's staring at you, especially since you're in the last row with the worst dancers, Ellen Kaplan and Maryann Gertz. And even if you do know the steps, your line looks wrong because Ellen and Maryann are always messing up, like doing a jété when it's supposed to be a glissade.

Even worse than crossing the floor is Parents' Day and crossing the floor. It's so bad that I don't really want to talk about it. I have noticed that if you talk about a thing, it gets more real.

Fara Snake Lynn makes me feel bad and stupid. My mother always says no one makes you feel anything, but I don't agree. My father, in this case, agrees with me because he thinks she's a snob. "Fara Lynn is a snob," he says, lifting his chin up and letting the words slide down the crooked nose he got when he fell down the front steps of a library in Brooklyn.

23

What I think about sadness is that basically it is difficult, and therefore not good. It makes your eyes puffy and your mother unhappy. She says, "Don't cry," or else she suggests, "Maybe you're tired, why don't you lie down?" Sadness is sort of like Diana Di Mitzio, the girl in my class I told you about who is not pretty and wears shabby clothes. No one really wants to play with her, but I try to be nice to her, like we used to say we would be in the Brownie pledge: "...to help other people at all times...." Diana Di Mitzio definitely needs help, and so once each week I make myself walk over to her, open my mouth and say, "Wanna play jump rope?" Suddenly Diana's eyes look like someone opened the refrigerator and there were cupcakes or something great inside and she says, "Sure!" and grabs my hand, which I don't like. We walk to the corner of the schoolyard and take turns with the rope. I'm better at jumping rope than she is, but that doesn't make me happy.

I wonder why people cry. I wonder if people cry more in Europe or in China than they do here. My mom has these handkerchiefs, which seem to be for crying; they have the letter "R" for Ruth on the corners, but she only uses them to pat her lipstick. And my dad's handkerchiefs—well he just blows his nose into them and makes a lot of noise. Except once, when we went to a movie called *The High and the Mighty*. It was about these people on an airplane that is definitely going to crash, and they know it. It was so scary that I sat on my hands because I felt like I was on the plane too. My dad was sitting next to me and he was making odd noises. When I looked over at him, there were tears, real ones—even in the dark I knew they were real. I didn't say anything, I just touched his leg for about one second, but I don't think he noticed because he was so sad. I think sadness does that—you don't notice things when it hits you, only it.

When I think about hungry people, kids especially, or when I think about dying, I get sad. Maybe angels will show up in the end, but who knows, and I can't help thinking about it. You have a bird, a parakeet, let's say, like we do, and then one day, *boom*, it's lying in its seed and *you-know-what* at the bottom of the cage right next to the water tray. No more little bites on the end of your finger, no more chirps, nothing.

It's like when you want to go somewhere really bad, like to the movies, but you're not allowed. Just at the moment when your mother says "No, absolutely not, company is coming to visit," or "No, it's not a good movie for kids," the exact moment you realize she really means it, you feel a kind of dying because what you really, really want is gone. Then there's being angry.

I remember how, a few years ago, I was playing "hit the penny" in front of the building and Linda got snotty. She put her stupid fist on her stupid hip, and stuck her tongue out at me. She was mad because I won three games in a row. Then she called me a dope really loud and, without thinking, I walked over and punched her in the stomach. Wham! She bent over like the cowboys do when they're shot in the movies, all dramatic, then she looked up at the sky and screamed. I looked up over her head at the sky too, but all I saw was two clouds.

"I swear," I told my mother, "I didn't mean it." She said, "Then why did you do it?" She got me clamped, her hands squeezing each of my arms to the sides of my chest. I was caught in her little jail. "Ouch," I tried, "I didn't mean to do it, my arm did it, it was an accident."

"Accidents don't grow on trees, " she said.

"I know that," I said, looking up at the skinny little maple nearby. There was nothing growing on it, not a leaf.

"We talk things out, we are not a violent family," she added as she let me go, then wiped the front of her blouse as if I got her dirty. I hadn't even touched her.

"Don't you do that ever again, you hear?" She shook her finger at me, like I was a dog, and I wagged my head up and down, like I was a dog. For a second I was thinking of barking, but I knew she'd go nuts if I did that. She might have even tied me to that little tree and said, "Every action has its consequences." So I didn't bark, instead I shook my head up and down politely...but what I was thinking was: *arf, arf, arf.*

Grown-ups have strange ideas about right and wrong, and a lot of it has to do with how things *look*. For example, you can smile nicely, let's say, at Aunt Gertie right after her terrible monster dog Rajah almost gave you a heart attack and you can, while you're smiling at her real sweetly, be thinking: "I hate you Aunt Gertie because you have a dog that wants to kill me and in fact, I wish your dog was dead, and any method would be okay by me—cars, or a shotgun, or cancer. Or maybe like in the French revolution with the guillotine." Anyway, you can think all kinds of terrible things and act nicely at the same time. What I mean is that the way things look can be fake. But my mother and most adults don't care; they want fake, they like it.

The truth is I liked punching Linda, and I know that sounds terrible and I'll probably never, even if I live to be 100, punch a person again, but: 1. She deserved it 2. I couldn't stop it, it was an instinct or something.

My teacher, Mr. Stein, says, "You're in charge of how you behave." Now, I like Mr. Stein but the truth is *he* is in charge of how we behave in school and if he said, get up and act like baboons, or moths, or sparrows, or Dracula, and our class really believed him, we'd have a great time thumping our chests, flapping our arms really fast near the lamp or in the air, or grunting and pretending to suck blood.

24

My father, what is he in charge of? Nothing I can see. He's not in charge of Negroes, although he likes them very much—don't ask me why. He also says he's an "agnostic," which means that he doesn't know if God is real or imaginary. I understand this because you can't see God, but you can see lots of other things, like pencils or trees. When he says he's agnostic, my father always points to the sky where there might be a cloud or an airplane, or nothing at all. I never see God there. I have tried experiments like watching Mrs. Bell get into her car, or saying, "God, if you're real, make my hair curly now!" Nothing happens. Or else I'll stretch out my hand and say, "God, if you're real, put a candy bar right here!" But again nothing. Then I think the problem is that I'm not important like Moses, so God doesn't hear me. Maybe if I tried talking to Him when I was in synagogue, He would hear me, but when I'm there I'm too busy talking to my friends.

Often, when my mother says something good has happened, or someone is better after being sick, she adds, "Thank God." But if the opposite thing happens, something bad, she doesn't say anything about God. My mother is positive God exists, but when I once asked her why, she said," I can't explain it." Then I said, "Well, it's like punching Linda Solomon," but she only wiped her hands on her apron, gave me a fake smile and said, "No it's not the same as punching Linda Solomon, it's very different," and she exaggerated the "very" by making the "e" part longer than it should be, which irritated me a lot.

So my mother believes in God, and my father doesn't, but my father sort of believes in Negroes. If God had brown skin maybe my father would like Him better. Also, brown-skinned people seem to have a better relationship to God, maybe because so many of them were brought over to be slaves and separated from their families, so they needed Him.

Negroes like to sing spirituals, which are all about God and wanting to go to Him, like *Swing Low, Sweet Chariot.* Maybe if I had to work so hard and got treated so badly, I'd want to be with God. I mean anything would be better than picking all that cotton, wondering where your mother is and being treated like a machine, something to be used rather than a human being.

One of the problems with my father liking Negroes so much is that we don't see them in our neighborhood. Hardly at all. Once, when I was wondering why my father rarely talks to me, I thought if I were a Negro he might be more interested, but I can't be because of my genes.

You should see him when Cynthia, the cleaning woman, arrives. She comes only one day every other week, and my father acts like she's the Queen of Sheba, he's so polite. Maybe he feels bad that she's cleaning our apartment. Anyway, sometimes grown-ups just don't act real. He makes such a big deal over her that it's embarrassing, and to make matters worse, Cynthia's shy. I can tell.

I know it's hard to like something so much and hardly ever see it, like me with Ricky Flaster, the boy I like from camp who lives in Manhattan. Or me and a cat. We're not allowed to have cats because of the furniture, "They scratch," my mother says looking down at our mahogany coffee table. Who cares? Well, she does and she's the boss.

ooo

Once my father was coming home from work and David Minton, Linda, Joey, and I were choosing sides for stickball. David was doing "Eeny, meeny, miny moe" and he said the "nigger" part just when my dad was coming up the walk. Dad heard me say to David, "It's not nice to say 'nigger,' say 'tiger.'" God, was he happy. He grinned and patted me on the head so much it hurt. But I could tell that he meant to show that he loved me. "Atta girl!" he kept saying, "Atta girl!" I liked it, but also I didn't because if it was just me he loved, not the me who believes all people are equal, but the whole me, I wouldn't have to say "tiger" for him to pat my head and say nice words. If I want him to love me more, I might have to help Negroes when I grow up because they are not allowed to do all the things I am—to live wherever they want and to get good jobs. I wonder how I would do that? I wonder how I would find them.

25

I don't have problems finding friends, the problem is that I have two best friends and I hate being in what my math teacher, Mr. Rheinish, explains is a triangle: three angles, three straight lines and lots of empty space in the middle. Carol equals one angle, Barbara another, and I'm the third. This may sound nice and orderly, especially if you picture an equilateral triangle, but it's a mess because someone is always feeling left out. The triangle, I think, is always nervous, like it wants to be a circle or a square. The Jewish star is two triangles—maybe that's what caused some of our problems.

Although my friends are girls, I seem to be more interested in boys lately although I hardly talk to them. Maybe that's what happens automatically in junior high school. Anyway, let's say it's three o'clock and we've finished comparing how many times the three of us each met Michael Shulman's eyes, and say Carol had three eye-clenchers, Barbara three and a half, and I had two, so I'm already feeling a little left out in the Michael Shulman department. Then, say, Carol is going over to Barbara's house and I have to go to the orthodontist to get my braces checked. I know we can't always be together, can't be equals all the time, but

I feel bad anyway. I imagine them in Carol's finished basement with chocolate chip cookies and milk, sort of doing homework and talking below that little wooden plaque that says, "Old golfers never die, they just lose their balls." Maybe they're saying nasty things about our class idiot, George Insana; maybe they are saying nasty things about me.

I like Carol better than Barbara because she's more interesting and so I don't always know what she'll say or do like I do with Barbara. Carol's dad is an artist and her mother is a socialist, maybe a communist even (Carol's not sure), so it makes sense that she'd be different. So Carol is the real source of my jealousy because I want her to like me better than she does Barbara.

When I think about all this, it reminds me of a story I heard once about a family in a boat—a mother, a father, and two kids. There's a storm up and not a lot of food left, so someone has to be thrown overboard or they'll all die. Jealousy is something like that, the feeling that your own mother, maybe, could throw you—not your sister—you, not your father— over the side of that boat. Just think about it and you know in your bones that you're just not the most special person in the world to someone, the most important before all others, which is what the rabbi says God wants you to feel for Him. "Thou shall have no other gods before me."

Maybe this need to feel special is natural. We are made in the likeness of God. Now I'm not saying that Barbara, my second-best friend, or Carol is God or anything, but it reminds me of the Bible. For example, when I think of how God wanted Abraham to kill his son Isaac for Him, I realize that even God, in all His glory, is insecure. Sometimes, when it really gets to me, I write Carol a letter and tell her how bad I feel, but then I don't send it. Instead I doodle on it, covering my shame with curlicues and flowers.

The real truth is that I know in my heart of hearts that Carol likes me better, it's just that sometimes I forget. It's like having faith. It's hard to have faith in the human race when you see how mean some people are, like making fun of Janet because she has polio, or treating Negroes like dirt. A lot of smart people are pretty stupid. A lot of smart people fall in love. I think pain might be the price of love. But Carol is not my boyfriend and all the sad rock-and-roll songs are about boyfriends, or girlfriends, depending on which you are. But since I haven't had a boyfriend yet, except for eye-clenchers with Michael, I don't know how to honestly compare loving a friend with loving a boy.

My mother says, "Do the labor great or small, do it well or not at all." But what is the labor of being a friend? What exactly do you do? It seems that if I work at it too hard, I feel bad and jealous. Why is that? I wish there were a boat big and strong enough for all of us so that no one ever had to be thrown overboard.

26

Along with junior high school comes camp, for the whole summer, and I really like it, even though it is so religious that you have to say Hebrew prayers almost every minute. In the morning it's *Mah To Vu*—"How goodly are thy tents O Jacob...." We're not even in Jacob's tents, we sleep in bunks. And what about Sarah? The prayers are all about men. And I never even met Jacob, although I know he's the famous man who wrestled with an angel. I did once meet Sammy Davis, Jr., who is also famous, not for wrestling, but for singing. Meeting him was so embarrassing. My mother, my sister, and I were walking down 34th Street in Manhattan on our way to Ohrbach's to buy new school clothes when we see three people walking toward us. They are Negro men, two tall ones and a short one in the middle.

"Oh, my God," my mother whispers really loud, "that's Sammy Davis, Jr."

"Who's that?" I whisper back.

"The singer, silly," she says as she frantically grabs me and Susie and drags us so we are standing right in front of him and his tall friends.

"Mr. Davis," my mother says in her high, nervous voice, "I love your music and I'd like you to meet my daughters, Genie and Susie." Mr. Davis is about my size, and when he smiles, his teeth are very white. Then the tall men smile down on us too, and Mr. Davis shakes first my mother's hand, then mine, then Susie's, and says, "Pleased to meet ya." Then he tips his hat, nods and the three of them sidestep us and keep on down the block. My mother holds her shaky hands in front of her chest, like she's trying to hold onto Sammy Davis, Jr. a little longer.

"That was wonderful," she says, beaming, still holding her left hand with the right.

There's no one famous at camp, only prayers, prayers, prayers. Before meals, a really long one. They put the Hebrew words to music to make it more fun, and I suppose it is a little better that way, but I'd rather sing along with the top ten on the hit parade on radio station WINS. At 7:30 they always play the number-one hit song in the country, and my dad always manages to come to the door of my room when I'm singing along and he always says, "How can you do your homework with that noise? Why don't you turn that junk down?"

"But Dad, it doesn't bother me, I told you," I tell him again. The little beige plastic radio is on my desk, it's 7:15, it's number four and counting down fast. He shakes his head and walks away.

What in the world do fathers think about? What is my peculiar father, in particular, really interested in? He always seems tired, not really grouchy, but like he'd rather be doing something else. But what? All men want sex, I read in a magazine once, but my father has a heart murmur and has to sleep a lot and anyway, and I can't and don't want to ever imagine my own mother and father doing that kind of thing.

But back to camp. What I like about it is not the kids in my bunk, especially not Joyce Feldman, the one who sticks tissues in her starter bra and parades in front of a small round mirror on a metal stand. It's too high for her chest, or anyone's, and so she stands on her tippy-toes, raises her arms over her head, and stares at herself as if she were a movie star or something. Maybe she thinks she *is* something, but I think she's stupid and insensitive.

I wonder who, or what, besides Joyce Feldman, is not sensitive? A mineral? A vegetable? I don't know. My mother always says, "You're too sensitive," but then she also says, "Be yourself." Pretty confusing.

ooo

One activity in camp is "Nature," which means a special counselor takes you into the woods and teaches you about the things there. The nature counselors always seem kind of creepy to me, unlike the dancing or swimming counselors. Sometimes I think the reason they are interested in nests and snakes and trees and flowers is because no one is really interested in them. Like Sandy. She labels and arranges all this nature stuff like it's gold, but it's just free junk that's all over the woods. You'd think it was her boyfriend's hair, the way she touches a robin's nest. And it's really a little disgusting because of the dried mud and crud in it. Once, when there was no scheduled activity and I was bored, I went to the Nature Shack and Sandy was sitting there crying. I started to leave, but she saw me and said, "No, Genie, come in...by all means." Who ever says, "by all means?" That's what I mean about nature counselors. I noticed a dead butterfly in her hand, a swallowtail. I knew because it had orange and blue at the bottom and was yellow and black everywhere else. She lifted it up for me to see with her two trembling hands, and so the wings shook even though it was dead.

"Pretty," I said.

"It's dead," she said, a tear running off her nose. I stood looking at her for a second, and felt strange, so I looked at the butterfly again.

I noticed caterpillars in jars, three of them in a row. There were sticks and leaves in with them too. "I gotta go," I said.

She nodded, put the butterfly down on the wooden table, and stood up. I was afraid she'd try to grab me because I was a live girl, but she just stood there and sighed.

"See you on Thursday," I said. I am an honor camper and so I know my schedule. Nature is always on Thursdays.

∘∘∘

My favorite counselor is Dani Dassa, who's Israeli and very cute. Cute doesn't usually go with big, but in this case it does. He once told me he has low blood pressure and is on the Israeli Olympic soccer team. He teaches us folk dancing, which is unusual for a man, but he's very good at it. Folk dancing is done in circles mostly, but some are done in couples, like Erev Shel Shoshanim, which means "Evening of Roses." Once I danced it with him and I nearly had a heart attack because I was in total heaven, and needed an angel's not a human heart.

I'm Dani's best student because I love dancing so much, and when you love things, it makes you naturally good at them. Or maybe you love them because you are good at them. Anyway, as I said, there are two kinds of Israeli dances, in couples or circles. Unless you're dancing alone with Dani, circles are the best because you can go faster and if you hold on real tight and make your feet do the right things, which is easy, you can go so fast that you feel "out of this world."

°°°

If you're twelve, almost thirteen, you know the difference between right and wrong. For example, it's wrong to kill people, or to hate them because of their skin color. It is right to be kind to people. There are ten commandments about these things, but most of them are for grown-ups because kids are too small to do them, like covet thy neighbor's wife.

Although it's natural, an instinct maybe, I can't help thinking it's wrong for animals to eat other animals. Like a snake eating a baby bird, which I saw happen outside my bunk when I was trying to write a postcard to my parents. And here's where love comes in at camp: it is absolutely wrong to accept a token of love from someone you don't even like. This is what happened:

This kid Harvey gave me his cap at camp. A cap is just a cap, but in this case it's more than a cap because it is a symbol. A symbol is when something represents more than itself—like an eagle is the USA or an "X" on a page means a kiss, or that your answer on the test is wrong. Whether it is a kiss or a wrong answer really depends on context clues. In any case, Harvey's cap was a symbol of how he liked me, the way a ring would be if I was older, and I'm very glad it wasn't a ring.

Why this Harvey likes me is a mystery since I never spoke a word to him in my entire life. He comes over to me at the dance in the social hall on Saturday night and makes a weird motion with his head and neck, like a slow tic or headache maybe and this means "Let's dance." Does he say, "Would you like to dance?" No. Does he offer me his hand like Rhett Butler in *Gone With the Wind*? No. Just this neck stuff, but I didn't want to hurt his feelings, so I danced with him, but I didn't like it. I didn't like how he smelled.

Now, I'm old enough to know what it's like to have a crush because I've had three of them: one on Michael Shulman who's in my class, one on Dani Dassa, the Israeli dance teacher at camp, and one on Tony Perkins, not in *Psycho*, but in *Fear Strikes Out*, a movie about a baseball player who has cancer. I am sure I do not have a crush on Harvey—he's littler than me, he's fat, and doesn't talk. I dance two bad dances with him, trying to keep my body as far away from his as possible, but then he takes my hand and kind of marches me to the kissing field. This is the dumbest thing at camp, dumber than all the prayers we have to say morning, noon, and night: all the boys and girls are allowed to kiss in the dark for five minutes before the boys get on the bus and go back to their side of the lake. What I imagine is that the boys think they have to kiss a girl and give her a cap so they're considered okay by the other boys. Kissing for kids our age is really dumb, but just walk into my bunk, find Joyce Feldman, the girl who puts tissues in her junior bra, and she will tell you I'm off base.

So here I am at the kissing field, but before Harvey can get his lips anywhere near mine, I begin to walk away. Then he runs after me and stuffs this blue and gold felt cap into my hand before I really realize what is happening.

ooo

I hate having it, it's worse than eating black licorice or liver. I put it in the back of my cubby, but I feel like I can see it back there, even in the dark. It's like it has a voice, a loud one. And, of course, Joyce, my evil, stupid bunkmate, has to broadcast this cap business out loud, "Genie and Harvey, Genie and Harvey," over and over.

Why didn't I just say no? Because I didn't want to hurt his feelings and it happened too fast. And now it will feel like three years until next Saturday night when I can return it. When things are going wrong in your life, time is very slow and wrong things gets bigger and bigger if you can't do anything about them.

Joyce says I'm crazy when I say that I'm giving Harvey back his cap.

"But it's great to have a cap," she says.

"Who says?" I snap.

"But everyone wants one, it means you're popular. Only six girls in the whole camp have them—Carol, Ellen, Brenda, Cora, me, and you."

°°°

Harvey hardly looks at me at all at the next dance. He just stands next to Gary Cohen, chews gum, and walks in and out of the social hall. I keep feeling the cap in the back pocket of my shorts. I keep talking to my friend Ellen trying to pass time and make the dance end.

When the counselors starts singing *Good Night Irene*, I know I'd better make my move. I will not bring that cap back to the bunk. So I wait for Harvey to leave, and as he's walking toward the bus, I run behind him, cough to get him to turn around, and put the cap in his hand. I want to explain, but I don't know what to say. He doesn't look surprised, he doesn't look anything really except short and fat. He doesn't say a word, just turns around and walks toward the bus.

I hope I didn't break his heart because I know he didn't cap anyone else that summer. I don't think I did, but who knows? Love is mysterious.

27

My mother always says that all she wants is for me to be happy and I don't want anyone to think I'm really a sad person, because I'm not. But the truth is that sometimes I'm sad. And you know what? Sad things are really more interesting than happy ones because what can you really say or think about nice, happy things? For example, you're playing a good game of stickball and you hit the ball thwack and off it goes, and you make a homerun, and your heart thumps and you feel, as my dad says, "like a million bucks." Now that's it, *it's great*, that's all you can really say. But when things are not great, when they are upsetting, it's much more complicated and they make you think hard because you have to try to figure them out in order to understand them and feel better.

Something happened at camp and I'm trying really hard to figure it out. I was standing on a hillside above the lake with a lot of the other girls waiting on line to take a canoe test. If you pass it, you get to go on a canoe trip on the Delaware River and sleep out overnight in a tent. It's a big deal and I really want to pass the test and go. We have buddies and I have Ellen, thank God, and not Joyce. As we're standing there, waiting and talking and swinging our towels and bathing caps, I see something terrible. Why I notice it and no one else does, I don't know—it's a baby drowning in the lake. You see, there's a swimming area by the shore below us under big trees for staff families, and some fathers and mothers are standing in the water up to their knees talking because most grownups like to talk more than they like to swim.

What happens next is that I see this little baby go under and come up like a strange toy in a bathtub, or one of those plastic birds my Aunt Yetta likes to attach to the rim of a glass so that its little head goes up and down, up and down.

Well, it's bad enough to watch a baby drowning, but it's worse to watch and not to do anything about it. I'm really ashamed to admit it, but I just couldn't do anything. I tried to call out, "Help!" or "Baby!" or "Look!" but nothing came out of my mouth. I've thought about this a lot because, as I said before, bad things make you do that, but all I can figure out is "peer pressure," which my social studies teacher, Mr. Rheinish, told us about. It means that kids want to be just like other kids and not to stand out and be different because they need to fit in and be accepted.

Anyway, so there I am up on shore, watching and feeling like a murderer. Thank heavens this story has a happy ending. The father, who was talking to another man, turns around after what feels like at least four years, sees the baby, picks her up out of the water, and puts her on his shoulder. All she does is cough a little and then she's fine. I even see her smile, so maybe she wasn't really drowning and it was, as they say, a figment of my imagination.

I bet you're wondering why this is such a problem since it all turned out happily ever after. Well, it's because I know that peer pressure is not as important as life and even if peer pressure is normal, I should have done something. I even have a Red Cross Junior Lifesaving Certificate. But I just stood there. And so all this business keeps stewing inside me and I keep thinking over and over that if I yelled, the yelling would have been better than silence. So what if the kids looked at me and thought I was crazy because I was wrong? I would have been trying to save a life.

28

Well here's something exciting! I can't believe it! I got it! I got it on the thirteenth day of September, which is thirteen days before my thirteenth birthday. Not only is it all these thirteens, but it's also the holy day we call Yom Kippur and so you're not allowed to eat. On this day you're supposed to fast, which means "starve," so that God will forgive you for all your sins and write your name down in the Book of Life for the next year.

I was fasting because my mother wanted me to. I can't really think of any other reason to feel so hungry on purpose... I mean what did I do that was so bad this year? All I can come up with is that I broke my mother's favorite vase, Selma Solomon's dish drainer full of dishes, and I knocked over the lamp stand with the donkey that has a planter on its back. You'd think I was that Indian god, the one with lots of arms, because I accidentally break so many things. "How can one girl destroy so much?" my mother asks. I shrug. "I'm sorry," I say. "You're so careless," she answers sadly, wiping her hands on her apron.

The day we fast, we also have to walk to the synagogue and back because you're not allowed to drive either and it's a long walk, maybe one whole mile each way. I walk back with my sister and Linda and Bonnie Solomon because our parents want to stay until sundown to pray and starve. Sometimes they get sips of water from the cooler outside the door to the special part of the synagogue where the ark and holy Torahs are. As I walk home, my stomach hurts more and more. It's a different kind of hurt than I've ever felt, but since this is the first time I'm fasting, I figure it's because of that. I start bending over as I walk so that I look like the old men in the temple with their shawls. They're always bending over like they have stomachaches. I wonder why, if they pray to God so much, they are so bent and miserable looking? Maybe it's because of Hitler.

My sister gets a worried look on her face, and Bonnie Solomon asks if I'm all right. "I'm okay," I mumble. When we get home, I sit in my father's green armchair and consider the situation: I am not thirteen yet, I am not confirmed. My stomach hurts so much I can hardly believe it. God won't mind if I eat.

"Do you think God would mind if I eat?" I ask my sister. She is ten and doesn't have to fast; she is eating sour cream and bananas. She says, "No, eating is okay," and licks the cream off her spoon.

"Do you really think so?" I say and she nods very seriously. I consider the problem again. I imagine asking my mother and her saying, "If you feel that bad, eat, eat." So I get some sour cream into a bowl, cut up a banana and mix it all together and dig in. Boy, does it taste good. The banana is soft and sweet and warm. The cream is cold and a little tart. My mouth is very, very happy. My sister, rinsing her bowl, tells me, "God will forgive you." How does she know? How does she know anything?

The bad part is that after I finish eating and go sit in my father's chair again, my stomach is still killing me, so I get up and go to the bathroom to examine it. I even poke and press it. Then I look down and see blood on my underpants. My heart starts beating like crazy and I get a big shiver, I think: This is it! *This is terrible!* I sit down on the toilet seat cover and call, "Somebody!!" My sister and Linda must be outside playing because Bonnie is the one who comes to the door. I open it about half an inch.

"I got it," I say in a whispery groan.

"*What* did you get?" Bonnie Solomon is my dumbest friend, she just proved it again.

"It…*it*. My period."

She sticks her head up into the door opening like she wants to see and I shut it fast. I bend over and hug my legs tight.

"You are so lucky," she yells, "Lucky, lucky, lucky!!!" Then she bangs on the bathroom door to make her point. "Lucky duck," she says, "I wish I had it."

"Take it!" I say, opening the door a crack again.

"Can I see?" she asks. I can see one of her beady eyes and some of her wild hair.

"Never!" I scream, and shut the door. Then I open it again. "Bonnie!" I yell, but I didn't need to because she was still standing right there.

"Don't you dare tell anyone, don't you dare," I hiss, and give her the look my mother has when she really means business.

"Cross my heart and hope to die," she says.

When I walk out of the bathroom, she stares at me like I'm Miss America or something.

"Stop staring!" I say, then I sit down in my father's chair again with my knees to my chest and hug tight. It helps a little.

°°°

When my mother comes home, I ask her to come into my room and I tell her: "I got my period and I had such a bad stomachache that I ate because I thought it hurt because I was hungry. Do you think it's okay? What about the Book of Life? I couldn't help it, if I knew before I ate, I wouldn't have eaten, but I only ate a little...." Mom gets a really nice look on her face and pats me on my knee. She's sits down next to me on my bed.

"I'm sorry you hurt so much," she says. "And now I have to slap you on the face. It won't hurt, I promise." So she takes the same nice hand that was just patting my knee, smiles, and hits me on my cheek! It's not too bad, just a little sting. "I had to do that," she explains, "it's a custom."

"What for?" I ask. This period business is peculiar.

"So that all the blood doesn't leave your body and make you pale."

Well, this makes no sense, not even a little. Lots of girls in my class already have their periods and they don't look pale. Being adult gets stranger and stranger the older you get.

My mother smoothes the front of her brown shiny dress and gets up. She's still wearing high heels because it's still the holiday. She goes out and comes back with a drink of water and some aspirin. I sit on my bed wishing I were ten years old again. Then she goes out and comes back with a brown paper bag, which she opens as she sits down next to me again. She takes out a little book called *What Every Girl Should Know,* and a white elastic thing with strange clips on it, and a pad named Kotex. Come to the bathroom," she says. Inside the bathroom, she sits on top of the closed toilet and I stand in front of her so she can fix me up. It's almost as bad as wearing head gear from the orthodontist, but it's on another place on your body and for a different problem. Thank God all this stuff isn't on my head.

I feel really queer with all this business on me: the elastic is tight and there's this big wad between my legs, which rubs when I walk.

"You'll get used to it," my mother says. She gives me a big hug and I can see, as she pulls me closer to her that her eyes are shiny and this is a big deal for her. I begin to feel better from her and from the aspirin. But through the whole day I keep feeling like I'm a big mystery to myself, which is very strange, but it's because I know I'm not the same girl I was before there was today. It's as if I suddenly had a different face, or a different name. But it's not either of these, it's my period, and it's my body doing what it is supposed to do even though it's doing this on the thirteenth day of September, thirteen days before my thirteenth birthday and thirteen is not a lucky number. Yet, in a queer way, I do feel lucky, even when my mother tells my father that I began to "menstruate" and my father, as usual, doesn't know what to say and looks down at the floor and mumbles, "Atta girl!"

Maybe I am lucky. But I hope my stomachaches, which my mother says are "cramps," won't be so bad next time, next month. And I sort of like the idea of the moon and me being kind of hitched up together now.

29

Soon after this excitement I have to go to my cousin Ira's bar mitzvah at a synagogue in Forest Hills. It's a fancy place, way fancier than our little temple, Beth Jacob. I have to get all dressed up. Ira wears a suit and he gets to stand at the *bima* and read his Haftorah. I know he worked very hard to get all that Hebrew straight and he did a good job, only stumbling four times over words and, when he did, his rabbi helped him out by moving the fancy silver pointer back to the line in the Torah and saying the words with him. I was sort of glad I wasn't Ira, but I was also mad. I worked just as hard as he did to become an educated Jew, and what did I get? A confirmation with eight other kids. We had to wear gowns, light blue ones, and then we stood before the congregation and recited Hebrew together. Rabbi Holtzer gave us each a tiny white Bible with gold on the edges of the pages and our names engraved on the covers under the words Holy Bible.

Only boys get to have bar mitzvahs, which mean they get lots of attention—a chance to be in front of the whole congregation alone, big parties, and loads of presents. But girls don't. I was good at Hebrew and was named the honor student. I think I have a feeling for God (even though it's confusing), given to me mysteriously, but I was still not able to stand at the *bima* and be the honored one. If a synagogue can't take a girl seriously, no wonder she has problems there.

Whether I'm pretty or not on the outside, when I grow up, I want to marry a man who is tall, handsome, and not fat. We will spend lots of time staring deeply into each other's eyes and be happy together forever. My mom and dad are okay, I mean they dance together after supper in the living room and sometimes hug and kiss, but I want more than that. Maybe I think I want more only because our apartment is so small—I mean it's so little that nothing tremendous can ever happen in it. Maybe if we lived in a jungle or a mansion, things would be more romantic. Maybe if my dad didn't have to go to work every day except Sunday, and if my mom didn't need to keep everything so tidy that she's always wearing a beat-up apron and carrying a rag in her hand. Maybe if she wasn't so busy opening and closing the venetian blinds because, God forbid, some sunlight might fade the fabric on the couch, or a neighbor might see something. What would they see? All we do here is the same ordinary stuff everyone else in this neighborhood is doing.

My husband, well—I think he'll look like Tony Perkins who is my idea of cute. I even wrote him a letter and he answered it: "Dear Gene: I'm glad you liked *Fear Strikes Out* so much. Your Friend, Tony Perkins." *Fear Strikes Out* is a movie about a baseball player who has cancer. Speaking of baseball, my friend Roz loves Sandy Koufax, the Jewish pitcher for the Brooklyn Dodgers. We once took three trains to Ebbetts Field to see him play and I had to listen to her sighing and screaming whenever he came out onto the field. In the sixth inning, a fly ball came right toward us, it even nicked the back of the seat right in front of me, but then it flew off. Just my luck. But if my true love were with me, he'd have gotten that ball for me, rubbed the dirt off it, patted it, and given it to me. He'd even have kissed my hand before he placed the ball in my palm, that's the kind of husband I want. Like Jacob who waited for seven years for Rachel because Rachel's father wanted her to marry his other daughter, Leah. My husband will be a nonconformist, like Holden Caulfield in *The Catcher in the Rye*, but not as crazy. I mean he'd see through phony stuff like Holden did, and that would make him exciting and different, but he'd be reliable. And when we'd speak, I wouldn't have to peel off layers of words to figure out what he meant, like you have to do with so many people.

Picture this: We'll fly to Europe on some kind of charter plane because they're cheaper. We'll hardly bring anything along because all that really matters is that we're together at the Seine or at Notre Dame or on our bed with wine and croissants and cheese. We'll stroll around arm in gentle arm and we'll gaze at each other over a little round table. We'll be drunk on love, staring into each other's eyes so hard that people will stare at us and be jealous.

Well, one problem I'm facing is finding this boy. I mean Junior High School 141 is okay, but most of the kids are, well, kind of simple and don't really understand people like me who love poetry, yearn to understand the nature of the universe, and cannot live on bread alone. I did like Michael Shulman, our eyes met between seven and ten times a day in the seventh grade and that was promising because the eyes, they say, are mirrors of the soul, but what happened was that when I finally got to talk to him, because we literally bumped into each other outside Mr. Stein's history class, all he could say was "hi" and the look in his eyes close up was pretty disappointing.

"Life is not a bed of roses," my mother said when she saw me after school that day. I must have looked disappointed. Even though my mother is always closing and opening and dusting the blinds, she's not dumb

"I know," I said sighing sadly. At least I don't feel really awful because of Michael Shulman, like Holden Caulfied did because of the whole world, but I was a bit depressed after all that promising eye contact. Maybe love is really blind, but if it is, I want it to blind me again and again, or have it take me into the fabulous forest where a tall, dark, and handsome hunter resembling Tony Perkins will pull me gently into his arms.

30

It seems that the older you get, and I'm thirteen now, the more questions you have, and the fewer of them can be answered by your parents, or anyone. It's like you've walked deeper into the forest of yourself and no one can find you, hear you, or tell you what's up. And a lot is up.

Not getting answers from God and your parents can be kind of disappointing, especially when you thought for a long time, like me, that if you asked a good question, you'd get a good answer. Plus, and this is an important plus, you thought the answer would be the truth. But what I've found is that when you get older and your parents no longer boss you around all the time because now you can do this to yourself, it gets really confusing. Who do you turn to and what is okay to ask? And by the time you get to my age, the really disappointing thing is that before you even ask your parents or a teacher a question, you already know what the answer will be and so you stop trying. To make it even worse, the questions, like the little lines your dad makes on the inside wall of the doorway with a ruler and pencil to show how tall you've gotten since the last time he did this, they get taller also. Soon the questions are taller than you are, and that's a lot to handle. So it seems to me, that as people grow up, they begin to ignore the big questions as much as possible, like they do my bratty cousin Robert. You learn just to smile at him from a safe distance, call out "Hi!" and give a little wave. Then you go somewhere else.

Sometimes I think it's a conspiracy, not asking questions or trying to find truth. At least that's how it is in our neighborhood. Maybe it's the whole world, but I don't know because I hardly ever leave here except to go to summer camp, and in terms of questions it's the same there. The

trees, which are beautiful, just stand in place, and don't, so far as I can tell, say a word, although maybe I'm not listening carefully enough. Now that I am "confirmed" I don't have to go to synagogue anymore, so I don't.

Sometimes I think I'm looking for God in the wrong place. When do I feel like something greater than me is in charge? I used to feel this with those "eye clenchers" with Michael Shulman, sometimes I do with books and poems when I'm swept away and something stronger than me takes over and I'm somewhere else even though I'm also here. It's hard to describe. Maybe God is a place between your body and somewhere else that is not death, but different from regular life. I really don't know. Maybe God is in your blood, but you don't feel or know it because, as they say, "we see through a glass darkly." When I'm really dancing, or singing or swimming, I'm also somewhere else. Is God there too? Sometimes I think I should just forget this entire line of questioning.

One night I was pretty upset because I'd just finished reading Anne Frank's diary for the third time and I couldn't stop thinking about it. That was one problem. The other had to do with how I said awful things about Bonnie Soloman. I told two girls and two boys that her I.Q. was 65. It really was—I looked it up in the school office when I was doing service for Mr. Stein. Then, to make it even funnier (or even worse, depending upon how you look at it), I said her I.Q. was lower than a vegetable's. Everyone thought that was a riot and the more they laughed, the worse I felt. To make it even worse, I had invited my friends, the ones I told about the low I.Q., over to one of my babysitting jobs and I'm not supposed to.

Later, after midnight, Mr. Minton finally drove me home and I was three dollars richer. Everyone in our house was asleep, everything was still except my mind, which was scurrying around inside of my head like a mouse. I was thinking of what I said about Bonnie. Then I thought that she would never know about it, so what was the big deal? I knew none of my friends were mean enough to tell her. So, I wondered again, Genie, what is the big deal? But it was a big deal. This went on and on so long that I decided to call on Mr. I-magination, like on TV. What I did was I pretend-

invited the rabbi, my mother, and my father into my bedroom, like a panel or a jury. It was a miracle because they all agreed to sit and answer any question I wanted to ask.

Rabbi Holtzer is in the middle with his kind face and big smooth forehead. Of course, he has his yarmulke on. Mom has dressed up for the occasion and looks pretty in a navy blue dress with big white buttons down the front. Her hair has its beautiful pompadour and you can see her pretty widow's peak. Dad is in his plaid shirt and regular pants. It's hard for him to sit still and so he's busy picking at his fingernails. I stand in front of them. My hair is in a neat ponytail and I have my penny loafers on without the pennies. I'm wearing a white blouse and dark skirt, nothing fancy.

I decide to start at the beginning. I put my hand on my chin and walk back and forth in front of the three of them like a lawyer. Since I don't whom to talk to first, I stop and face all three.

"I have some important questions," I begin, "and I think you are the ones I should address them to. I won't beat around the bush, I'm really confused about some important things. For example, how do you really know what is good from what's bad, the difference...?"

The first thing I notice is that my dad rolls his eyes a little, then he's back to his cuticles. My mom shifts in her seat. I know she won't say anything to begin with because the rabbi is next to her and she is religious. Rabbi Holtzer looks side to side, gives a little shrug, then stares at me.

"Could you repeat your question please, Genie, dear?"

"How do you know what is good from what is bad?"

"Ah," he says, leaning back, "Ethics, ethics. It is good a child should consider such things."

He closes his eyes for a few seconds, opens them and says, "And why do you ask?"

"Because sometimes it's hard to tell."

"Well," he says, glancing at my mom and dad on either side of him. "There are, of course, the Ten Commandments."

"Yes," I tell him, "I know them from Hebrew school, but they don't cover everything—like saying mean things about other people."

My mother tilts her head to see if the rabbi is finished or not. He nods to her.

"Well," she says, putting her elbows on the table, you remember what I always say: 'Do unto others as you would have others do unto you.'" I can tell that she is proud of me for asking. My father nods, the rabbi nods.

I consider this. The problem is that I've heard these words so many times, like *please, thank you, excuse me*, it's like an old Bartlett quotation. "Lackluster," my English teacher would say. The other problem is this: how do you know what you "would have" others do unto you? What would you really like from them? It all depends. If Michael punched me on the arm like he did Barbara once, I'd really have liked it because it might have meant that he had a crush on me. But if anyone else did, I'd hate it because I'm a pacifist. It's like in reading comprehension: you need the context clues. What you want others to do always depends on the situation, and that changes all the time. How will I ever explain this to the grown-ups?

I start trying to explain, but stop. I can't tell them about my old crush on Michael Shulman, or about what I'd said about Bonnie Solomon to the other kids. There is a long silence. The rabbi nods to my mother and then looks over at my father who is looking at me. It begins to be really embarrassing.

"You are a very intelligent girl," the rabbi finally says. My mother nods vigorously. "It is good that you are filled with questions. A thoughtful young person is a blessing."

Me? A blessing? This meeting is not working out well. Maybe one more try. . . .

The rabbi and my parents keep staring at me.

"How can God be good, be a good God, with so many terrible things in the world? If He is so powerful, wouldn't he be nicer to people and not make them suffer so much? This really confuses me."

"Ah," the rabbi says, "the problem of Job. Such a deep girl. It is a wonderful thing."

I stand there patiently, the light in my imaginary room now fading into gray. No one says a word. The rabbi keeps on smiling, my mom stares at her hands, my dad's eyes scan the ceiling.

"Dad," I say, "What are you thinking?" He could at least try.

He shrugs his shoulders, then rubs his black onyx ring on his shirtsleeve and looks into it. "Each person carries within him the world in which he must live," he says.

So that's what my father thinks! Maybe that's why he hardly ever says anything—maybe he thinks the world he carries within him is so different from other peoples' worlds that it's not worth trying to explain.

"An interesting theory," the rabbi offers and shakes my father's hand.

My dad likes this, I can tell. Meanwhile, my mother gives me a little wave, and I wave back at her.

"I guess that's it," I say and then the three of them give each other sideways glances back and forth like the contestants do on *What's My Line?* before the real guy stands up. But this time the three of them get up at once, disappear, and I am in my room alone. I hear a car pass by in the street, see its headlights scour the ceiling.

"*Che sera, sera,*" I hum in Italian, or is it Spanish? I

decide there are a lot of places to go, with or without my questions. There is ice-skating and poetry and there is the Hit Parade and a boy out there who will someday love me. There is a God of some sort, and so what if it takes forever to figure it all out?

That night I dreamed I was in a rowboat and I had two oars, a big bag of tunafish sandwiches, and three oranges. The waves were rocking me this way and that, but my questions and I were just fine out there, really.